At a time when the instituti[on] under threat from multiple [sources,] a biblical view of its divine o[rigin] our eyes above the day-to-day [...ties] or maintaining healthy marriages and see God's grand and beautiful design for marriage, which is far higher and greater than merely our happiness in this world. This book does both with a remarkably comprehensive tour of the Bible's teaching on marriage. If ever a book earned its title, this one did, as I closed its pages *Lost in Wonder*.

DAVID MURRAY
Pastor and Professor, Puritan Reformed Theological Seminary,
Grand Rapids, Michigan

There are many Bible overviews that trace God's plans through Scripture. Lost In Wonder explores God's passion, his proposal. From Genesis to Revelation we see the triune God's unstoppable marital love for we unworthy recipients. Read this book to grasp not only the heart of the Scriptures but the heart of God.

GLEN SCRIVENER
Evangelist, Speak Life, Eastbourne, East Sussex, England

That the powerful king of the universe is a God of passionate love makes for glorious biblical theology. That he would relentlessly pursue a sinner like me in such love is simply mind-blowing. But the apostle Paul wanted his readers to grasp this truth deep down (Eph. 3:18-19), and so does Peter Mead in his moving new devotional. Read, reflect and be lost in wonder.

DAVE GOBBETT
Lead Minister, Highfields Church, Cardiff, Wales

We all hunger for great relationships. This wonderful book by Peter Mead talks about our greatest and most important relationship ever. Our relationship with God himself. There is a place in our heart for God that absolutely nothing else can satisfy. Read this book with an open heart and let your hunger for His grace and presence grow.

LEIF NUMMELA
Author & Bible Teacher, Finland

LOST IN WONDER

A Biblical Introduction to God's Great Marriage

PETER MEAD

CHRISTIAN
FOCUS

Copyright © Peter Mead 2016

paperback ISBN 978-1-78191-907-1
epub ISBN 978-1-78191-917-0
mobi ISBN 978-1-78191-918-7

10 9 8 7 6 5 4 3 2 1

Published in 2016
by
Christian Focus Publications Ltd,
Geanies House, Fearn, Ross-shire,
IV20 1TW, Great Britain.

www.christianfocus.com

Cover design by Moose77.com

Printed and bound
by
Bell & Bain, Glasgow

CONTENTS

Acknowledgements

Surely no book can be the work of just one writer. This one certainly is not. What I share here has been shown to me over many years by many teachers and preachers. I still thank God for the years I was able to spend studying the Bible at Multnomah Biblical Seminary. Ideas that come out in this book first 'came in' during classes there sitting under the teaching of Bruce Fong, Al Baylis, John Terveen, John Wecks, and Ron Frost. I have gained so much from working alongside Ron Frost in Cor Deo, especially on the themes of this book.

I also want to mention Mark Stirling, Dane Ortlund, Glen Scrivener and Leif Nummela for their contributions in single conversations that were so helpful. David Searight was a big help with historical sources as well as various biblical insights while co-labouring at Cor Deo. I am thankful for the encouragement of Mike Reeves, and especially Mike Chalmers, as well as the people of Trinity Chippenham who have heard many of these ideas in sermon form over recent years. It has been great to work with the folks at Christian Focus again on this project. A big thank you to Ray Ortlund, Jr., not just for writing the foreword to this book, but for your writing on this subject that has been such a help to me. I hope your new book on the subject is a huge success.

Last but not least, a huge thank you to my wife Melanie, not just for great help with editing this book, but mostly for so consistently showing what it looks like to honour Christ in marriage. Naturally this book is dedicated to my bride – by God's grace I married out of my league.

Foreword

If we perceive Christianity in only behavioral categories, it might seem tedious and smug. To be sure, we do find moral elegance, with an edge of urgency, pervasive throughout real Christianity. It is not a flippant approach to life. But what if the message of Christianity is far more? What if the heart of Christianity is about a love too great to be limited to what we deserve morally? What if the message of Christianity speaks of a love so vivid and intimate and personally desirable that we might find it unsettling when it gets up close to us? What if the passion within Christianity is not our passion for God, which is weak, but God's passion toward us, which is intense? What if the loving intensity burning in the heart of God is romantic in nature? What if, as we look around in this world for metaphors for divine love, the human love of marriage gives us one of the clearest insights? What if we have been wrong in some of our most basic thoughts about God? What if, more than God the Ultimate Lawyer, the Christian gospel is telling us about God the Ultimate Lover? Finally and most amazingly, what if God, rather than choosing the beauty queen, passes her by and deliberately chooses the whore and woos her – that is, us – with a sincere tenderness directly relevant to the deepest longings of our broken hearts?

This new book by Peter Mead, *Lost in Wonder: A Biblical Introduction to God's Great Marriage*, invites us all to rethink our perception of God with fresh categories. Fortunately, this new way of thinking about God is not our own wishful thinking. Far better, it comes straight from the Bible and is illustrated here with relevant quotations from outstanding Christian thinkers from previous centuries. What you are holding in your hands is a book that might change not just this or that thought about God but the whole way you think of God and feel about him. The truths explained here have certainly changed me, and I will never go back to the legalistic religion I used to lug around.

Peter Mead is a pastor and mentor with deep insight into the glorious vision of God revealed in the Bible. Peter thinks carefully and studies responsibly. He can be trusted. Some of the themes he brings out of the Bible are hard to accept. But that only validates Peter more, since he is not picking and choosing but is facing what the Bible actually says. For example, if God is the Ultimate Lover, then we have to change how we think of our sins. Sin is not breaking a petty rule; sin is wounding God's tender heart. But the good news is that the One we all betray is faithful. Indeed, God is more faithful than we are sinful. Peter has written this book to help us stare at that astounding reality long enough for our hearts to crack open to God.

Maybe the best way to take advantage of this book is to read it at an unhurried pace. (Who of us these days doesn't need to slow down, anyway?) So, rather than speed-read this book, you might enjoy it more a few pages at a time – like a piece of hard candy that you pop into your mouth and roll around with your tongue and let it melt there for a while. A book like this, savored like that, might become for you that rare experience – a book that leaves an impression deep enough to last a lifetime.

RAY ORTLUND, JR.
Pastor, Immanuel Church,
Nashville, Tennessee

Introduction

Surely the bubble has burst. The fairytale of married happily ever after seems to have failed for too many of us. This is a book on the marriage of God to His people, rather than advice for human marriage, but nonetheless it is a book that will mention marriage on almost every page. You may be wondering why you are even looking at it. Is this going to rub salt into your wounds and make you feel bad about your situation? I hope not.

After writing the book I considered putting an appendix in, called 'When Marriage Hurts.' I thought it would be good to be sensitive to those who find marriage to be a painful subject. Then I decided to put it up front. There are simply too many people wounded by marriage today.

Maybe your parents' failed marriage still hurts you today, even though the break-up may have occurred decades ago.

Maybe you are still single and have grown disillusioned and discouraged that you are still alone in life. Maybe you are or have been married, but you have been betrayed, neglected, or abused. Maybe you have been the betrayer or the one who has taken most of the blame. Perhaps you appear to have a happy marriage, but know that on the inside it is disappointing on a daily basis. Perhaps the tension with your spouse, or perhaps relational distance, although not obvious to others, is very painful for you.

Ever since we humans curved in on ourselves in the Garden of Eden, marriage has been difficult, to say the least. Instead of two selfless beings giving themselves to each other, we default to the new normal: two self-concerned individuals negotiating an arrangement that tends to serve self as the primary concern.

Marriage can, and often does, hurt us very deeply. That is because marriage is so central to God's design for humanity. When the things that we were designed to enjoy most let us down, then they hurt us the most.

Perhaps the pain you feel is not a reason to put this book down, but a reason to keep reading.

This book is not about human marriage, but in a strange way, it is. In this book we are going to travel through the Bible to see God's great plan for God's great marriage. And the wonderful thing is that God's great marriage is not about God getting something we can't seem to successfully get for ourselves. God's great marriage involves us. The invitation, the proposal, is to us!

Whatever our experience of marriage might be in this life, each of us is invited to enjoy the greatest marriage both in this life and in the one to come. This book might help you in respect to your human marriage, but that would be a side benefit. The goal is to lift our eyes to the marriage that every other marriage is supposed to point towards. As we glimpse this divine marriage, we see something captivatingly glorious, something that offers hope to lift us beyond any experience this evil world might throw our way. I pray it will lift us into the embrace of the Perfect Bridegroom Himself.

If you have been hurt by marriage, then my prayer is that this book might offer healing, perspective, and hope. Actually, no book can really do that because the wounds typically go too deep. But the Bridegroom can. I pray He will.

- -

Every June my wife and I celebrate our wedding anniversary. It is a special day, so naturally we will set the table with a special tablecloth, some candles, put on some gentle background music and enjoy a nice meal. As we hold hands we can't help but gaze together at the marriage certificate that takes pride of place at the centre of the table. Hold on, that doesn't sound too romantic! Actually, that would be bizarre, wouldn't it?

To celebrate a marriage by focusing primarily on the legal reality represented by the contract would be strange, to say the least. Sadly, I suspect many Christians do this all the time. Not necessarily with human spouses but with Christ, our groom.

The Bible makes marriage its pre-eminent image for our relationship with Christ, but too easily we seem to turn that into a celebration of a legal status change, while missing out on the greatest privilege of all – being one with Christ. For many in our churches today, a Christian life has diminished into a merely legal version of salvation – that by faith in

Christ we have a new status before God. When we chase through the Bible and see how rich the marital theme is, I can't help but wonder why we have been so captivated by a reduced gospel.

Christianity does not offer us just a status change. It is not simply that we were sinners who now have been legally justified in God's eternal records. Nor are we offered a relationship with Christ that is somehow *like* a marriage. Rather, Christianity offers us the wonder of being one with Christ, of being married. That includes and requires some legal realities, primarily justification. These legal realities are, indeed, very important. However, being one with Christ also includes relational realities: communication, companionship, and relational intimacy, all in the context of a true spiritual union. When we dare to scratch at the surface of Christianity with our noses in our Bibles, we discover the most astonishing reality that will thrill our souls for the whole of eternity – we are invited to be one with Christ!

Almost exactly five centuries ago, a feisty young German scholar became so gripped by this good news that through him God turned Europe upside down with the message. Before we preview what is coming in this book, let's take a moment to ponder some of Luther's writings. Here's an extended quote from Martin Luther's *Freedom of a Christian*, published in 1520:

> The third incomparable benefit of faith is that it unites the soul with Christ as a bride is united with her bridegroom. By this mystery, as the Apostle teaches, Christ and the soul become one flesh [Eph.5:31-32]. And if they are one flesh and there is between them a true marriage – indeed the most perfect of all marriages, since human marriages are

but poor examples of this one true marriage – it follows that everything they have they hold in common, the good as well as the evil. Accordingly the believing soul can boast of and glory in whatever Christ has as though it were its own, and whatever the soul has Christ claims as his own. Let us compare these and we shall see inestimable benefits. Christ is full of grace, life, and salvation. The soul is full of sins, death, and damnation. Now let faith come between them and sins, death, and damnation will be Christ's, while grace, life, and salvation will be the soul's; for if Christ is a bridegroom, he must take upon himself the things which are his bride's and bestow upon her the things that are his. If he gives her his body and very self, how shall he not give her all that is his? And if he takes the body of the bride, how shall he not take all that is hers?

… Thus the believing soul by means of the pledge of his faith is free in Christ, its bridegroom, free from all sins, secure against death and hell, and is endowed with the eternal righteousness, life, and salvation of Christ its bridegroom.

… Who then can fully appreciate what this royal marriage means? Who can understand the riches of the glory of this grace? Here this rich and divine bridegroom Christ marries this poor, wicked harlot, redeems her from all her evil, and adorns her with all his goodness. Her sins cannot now destroy her, since they are laid upon Christ and swallowed up by him. And she has that righteousness in Christ, her husband, of which she may boast as of her own and which she can confidently display alongside her sins in the face of death and hell and say, 'If I have sinned, yet my Christ, in whom I believe, has not sinned, and all his is mine and all mine is his,' as the bride in the Song of Solomon [2:16] says, 'My beloved is mine and I am his.'

MARTIN LUTHER, 'The Freedom of a Christian'[1]

Luther was a Bible man, and what he found in the Bible thrilled his soul and filled his heart. The whole story of God's great plan from eternity to eternity can be traced via three 'unions.'

First, there is the beautiful union of God: Father and Son bound together in glorious, selfless love by the Holy Spirit. Tour the planet and survey history, you will never find a god that comes anywhere near to the beauty and wonder of the one true God! As a student of Luther's writings and English Puritan, Richard Sibbes explained, out of the spreading goodness of that beautiful communion came creation and, subsequently, redemption.

Second, there is the remarkable union of God and man in the Incarnation. God the Son took on flesh and dwelt among us – to make God known, to draw people to Him, and to take away the sin of the world. It has been said many times, but you need Christmas to get to Easter. He was pleased to dwell with us. Angels scratch their heads in wonder, and so should we.

Third comes the breath-taking union between Christ and His church. Because He came, because He died and lives again, because of the atonement, we are now invited to have union with Christ. Not just sins forgiven (which would be wonderful), but also to be given new hearts and united to

---

1. Martin Luther, 'The Freedom of a Christian' in *Three Treatises* (Fortress Press, 1943), pp. 286-7.

Christ by the Spirit God has now given to us. Salvation would be mere legal pardon from a benevolent deity if it weren't for the wonder of these three unions – The Trinity, the incarnation of Christ, and now our own union with God. Beautiful. Remarkable. Breath-taking.

This book begins before things began. We will venture into holy territory as we catch a glimpse of the first of these three unions – the beautiful union of God the Trinity. Part one does what the Bible does, it quickly moves on into the mess of this sinful world. As we progress through the books of Moses we will discover the distance between God and man, the way we as humans fall short of God's marital ideal.

By the way, before each chapter you will find a quote or two related to the book's subject. Some of the sources will be familiar to you. Others may not. Either way, be encouraged to chase those books and authors to enjoy more of their writings. The goal of this book is to introduce you to the Bible, but if it can introduce you to other books too that will feel like a win for me.

In part two we will take a tour of the rest of the Old Testament. We will see kings and paupers, prophets and prostitutes. We will see the tragic confusion we creatures like to create for ourselves, but we will also glimpse the growing hope of a great marriage that flows from an ever faithful God.

In part three we will meet Him, the groom: Christ Jesus. The second great union is that between God and man in the person of Christ. So we will spend some chapters fixing our eyes on Him. We will watch the miracle of His arrival, listen to His perspective on marriage, see Him wooing His bride, and watch Him make the proposal. In Jesus, God comes to humanity, so that humanity might be brought to God … the wonder of the Christian message!

Finally, in part four we will ponder the third great union – the unspeakable privilege of Christ and us becoming one. This reality absolutely astounded the apostles, as we will see when we listen to Jesus' half-brother, watch persecutor Paul marvel over union with the Messiah, and finish with the beloved disciple as he anticipates the fulfilment of all God's plans.

The Bible begins with a wedding, and it will end with one. Is it possible to put into words what the climax of the Bible will be like? We will try. As we come to the conclusion of the book we will lift our vision beyond time and hopefully we will be stirred to lift our hearts in prayer:

> Finish then, thy new creation;
> Pure and spotless, let us be;
> Let us see thy great salvation,
> Perfectly restored in thee:
> Changed from glory into glory,
> 'Til in heaven we take our place,
> 'Til we cast our crowns before Thee,
> Lost in wonder, love and praise! [2]

The great wedding is coming, and if we are His, then we will be there. Marriage is not just a good illustration of something essentially different, it is actually God's heart for union with us being revealed through time and into eternity. As we move through this book together, my prayer is that we will catch a glimpse, that we will be changed, and that He will be pleased!

---

2. Charles Wesley, 'Love Divine, All Loves Excelling', Hymn, 1747.

Part One

What Kind of God, What Kind of Creatures?

Pay attention only to this Man, who presents Himself to us as the Mediator and says: 'Come to Me, all who labor, etc.' (Matt. 11:28). When you do this, you will see the love, the goodness, and the sweetness of God. You will see His wisdom, His power, and His majesty sweetened and mitigated to your ability to stand it.[1]

MARTIN LUTHER

---

1. Martin Luther, *Lectures on Galatians,* 1535 edition in *Luther's Works,* vol. 26 (Concordia, 1963), p. 30.

The Beautiful Union of God

• JOHN 17

God *is* a mystery, but not in the alien abductions or things-that-go-bump-in-the-night sense. He is certainly not a mystery in the 'who can know, why bother?' sense. God is a mystery in that who He is and what He is like are secrets, things we would never have worked out by ourselves. But this triune God has revealed Himself to us. Thus the Trinity is not some piece of inexplicable nonsense like a square circle. Rather, because the triune God has revealed Himself, we can know the Trinity. That is not to say we can know everything about God. To know the Trinity is to know God, an eternal and personal God of infinite beauty, interest and fascination. We *can* know God the Father through the Son by the Spirit, and we can forever grow to know Him better.

What we assume would be a dull or peculiar irrelevance turns out to be the source of all that is good in Christianity. Neither a problem nor a technicality, the triune being of God is the vital oxygen of Christian life and joy.[1]

MICHAEL REEVES

We live in a rapidly changing world. But the biggest question each of us needs to answer remains the same: which god is God? Perhaps we haven't really thought about this, but that would make us unusual. Most people, in most places, for most of time, have known that there are multiple 'god options' on the religious menu. It is a relatively small number of people in a limited region of the globe that think they automatically know who God is. But do they?

Which god is really God? What is this God like? How can we know? The Bible is God's self-revelation to us. As we turn its pages and read the unfolding story we are gradually introduced to God. If He didn't choose to reveal Himself to us, then we would be groping around in the dark. We would be making up our own explanation for everything. And for thousands of years, that is exactly what people have done.

If you tour the world and survey history, you will encounter countless deities. Some may be more attractive than others. Some seem hideous, and others petty. What you won't find is a god like the God of the Bible. Why? Because when fallen humans try to make sense of everything, we will always default to doing what Feuerbach described as 'projecting our own ego onto the clouds'.[2] The gods we imagine will tend

1. Michael Reeves, *The Good God* (Milton Keynes: Paternoster, 2012), pp.ix-x, xvi.
2. Lesslie Newbigin, *The Light Has Come* (Grand Rapids, Eerdmans: 1982), p107.

to be beings just like us, but pumped up on steroids. The problem is that we are fallen creatures with a twisted and upside-down understanding of reality. It is understandable that our divine guesswork will always be a corruption of the true God.

So we come to the Bible. God is not defined on a specific page. When you have read the whole thing you will feel like you have just begun. In fact, eternity will not be long enough to fully come to know God. But there is good news. He has been made known.

God wants us to know Him, and He has done what it takes to make Himself known. As we read through the Bible we read of prophets sent from God to speak His word. But then we come to the New Testament and we meet the ultimate revelation – Jesus Christ, the Son of God. Philip, one of Jesus' followers, once asked to see the Father. Jesus' answer reverberates through history: 'Whoever has seen me, has seen the Father.' (John 14:9)

Earlier in John's gospel we are told that no one has ever seen God. But the only God, who is at the Father's side, He has made Him known. (John 1:18) When we see Jesus, we see the fullness of the Godhead dwelling bodily. When we encounter Jesus interacting with His Father, then we are truly on hallowed ground.

There are three occasions when God the Father speaks from heaven in the Gospels. There are several occasions when God the Son speaks to His Father in heaven, but one extended occasion. Let's look at these briefly:

The Baptism of Jesus

Jesus came to His quirky cousin John the Baptizer, to be, well, baptized. This was the moment that Jesus 'went public' in His ministry as the Messiah. It was a big moment! Jesus had become a human three decades earlier, but now He stepped into the waters to identify with the sinful people God was calling to turn back to Him.

As Jesus emerged from the water, the Gospels tell us that heaven was opened, the Spirit came down on Him and a voice spoke from heaven. This was not an everyday occurrence! In fact, this was a very special moment in history. God's voice was actually heard in our realm. And what did He say? Did He speak of His own power, position, authority? Did He reveal His plans or moral instruction? No. He spoke about His Son!

'This is my beloved Son, with whom I am well pleased.' (See Matt. 3:13-17.) In fact, Mark and Luke record the words being addressed to Jesus, 'You are my beloved Son; with you I am well pleased.' (See Mark 1:9-11; Luke 3:21-22.)

We live in this world and need a voice from outside to make sense of it all. Heaven was ripped open and God's voice boomed down. He spoke of His love for His well-pleasing Son. Does that seem like an anti-climax? Or is it, in fact, a glorious glimpse into a reality that is wonderfully different from this self-absorbed world that we are so used to?

The Transfiguration

Later on in His ministry, Jesus took three of His closest followers with Him on to a mountain. Suddenly their this-world perspective gave way to another glorious glimpse of heavenly reality. Jesus was transfigured before their eyes and they fell to the ground. Jesus was suddenly not 'veiled' but gloriously visible to them. Jesus was radiating celestial brightness while having a conversation with Moses and Elijah.

The disciples grasped for something appropriate to say. They ended up with a very 'this-world' thing to say ... 'it's good for us to be here,' and 'let's build some temporary shrines (since you three are so powerful)!' Oops. They were missing the point. So God spoke again.

Again God spoke and introduced His Son. Again God spoke of how pleasing the Son was to Him. This time He told them to 'Listen to Him!' The same instruction given a millennium and a half earlier when God foretold the coming of the Prophet like Moses was now spoken with a present tense point of reference. When we get a glimpse into heaven we discover a world shaped by a Father delighting in His Son who is pleasing to Him. Strange? Or strangely attractive? It's just a glimpse, but there is something about it that should warm our hearts. (See Matt.17:1-9; Mark 9:1-8.)

Some Said It Thundered

As Jesus approached Jerusalem for that first Easter, a voice came from heaven for the third time. This time the crowds were there again, and some Greek folks approached the disciple with a Greek name (Philip) and asked to be introduced to Jesus. Philip and Andrew brought the request to Jesus and suddenly Jesus launched into the most obscure of apparent non-answers. (See John 12:20-36.)

Suddenly Jesus is talking about being glorified, and that His hour had come. (*Yes, Jesus, that's good, but what about the Greeks?*) And He carried on into a farming analogy – a grain of wheat needs to die and be buried in order to bring forth a crop. (*Right, Jesus, but what about the Greeks...?*) And so people need to be ready to lay down their lives in service of Christ. (*Lay down their lives, right, got it, but what about the Greeks?*)

Next thing we know Jesus is getting distressed and He cries out in prayer to His Father, asking Him to glorify His name. Don't miss verse 28. God replied, 'I have glorified it, and I will glorify it again.' Amazing.

Jesus continued, talking about judgment. (*Judgment coming, good. But anyway, the Greeks?*) Jesus finally answers the question, 'When I am lifted up from the earth I will draw all people to myself.' There it is. God has been glorified in the person of His Son, and He will soon be glorified again in the Son, and the Son will draw people from all nations to Himself … and amazingly, it is all about Jesus dying on that cross. Somehow God is glorified in the Son's death. Somehow that is the hour of Jesus' glorification. Somehow we don't quite see the world clearly from where we are standing.

Three times God speaks from heaven, and now we get to really listen in as Jesus speaks to His Father. Take off your sandals, we are entering John 17 …

The Prayer of Jesus

In this remarkable prayer Jesus makes seven requests. The first two come in the first section, where He is praying about His own mission to give eternal life, which means to know God and His Son (vv. 1-8). He wants the Father to glorify Him so that He can glorify the Father in return (v. 1). He wants to return to what He had before the world existed – a shared glory in the presence of His Father (v. 5).

Now we are glimpsing eternity past. Before anything was, what was there? Before planets and people, before mountains and mobile phones? There was God. And what was He doing?

To listen to some people, you'd imagine that God was planning how to rule everything, or what laws to establish, or perhaps He was looking in the mirror checking how good

He looked, or how strong He was. But wait, that sounds like ego-projection again, that sounds like a projection of us on some kind of spiritual steroids.

No, before the world existed, there was God. The Father was lovingly glorifying the Son, and the Son was responding by glorifying the Father. They were sharing glory together. This is a gloriously attractive reality!

From verses 9-19, Jesus continued to pray for the disciples that had been given to Him. He was concerned for them, as revealed in His next three requests: 'Holy Father, keep them in your name,' (v. 11) and 'keep them from the evil one,' (v. 15) and 'Sanctify them in the truth; your word is truth' (v. 17). Jesus was concerned for these vulnerable disciples in an antagonistic world, and so He prayed for them.

Then we come to the final verses of the chapter, verses 20-26. If this chapter is hallowed ground, then these verses are the Holy of Holies. Now we find Jesus praying for those who will believe in Him because of the word of the disciples. He was praying for us!

There are two requests remaining, what are they? He prayed that 'they may all be one, just as you, Father, are in me, and I in you, that they also may be in us, so that the world may believe …' (v. 21) Really? Christian unity? Isn't that just a minor pragmatic concern? Surely He should be reaching a crescendo here? Actually, He is. Notice the kind of unity He prays for – a 'just as' kind of unity, just as the Father and Son share together. Now that is a big ask, and since it is asked at such a big moment, it must also be a big deal in the heavenly way of viewing things.

Jesus goes on to pray about how He has shared His glory so that believers would become perfectly one, again so that the world will know about God sending the Son. And there's more: that the world might know that the Father Himself loves us even as He loves the Son. That right there is enough to make you put the book down and pray for a while. Even as? Really?

Now we see the final request, and in the process, we catch the most precious glimpse into the Trinity. Jesus prayed, 'Father, I desire that they also, whom you have given me, may be with me where I am, to see my glory that you have given me because you loved me before the foundation of the world.' (v. 24) Jesus wants us to be with Him so we can see His glory. This isn't a selfish request; He really wants to show off His Father's gift to Him. But don't miss that critical link, that glorious glimpse into what godly glory is all about … 'Because you loved me!' God glorifies His Son because He loves Him! Love drives true godly glory.

John 17 is the greatest and most glorious glimpse into the relationship at the heart of the cosmos. God is not self-absorbed. He is others-centred. God is not a grabber of glory, but within the perfection of the Trinity each Person is wonderfully glory-giving to the other. God is not primarily obsessed with His own power, but rather He delights to love and glorify and give.

Tour the world today, and travel through time as well, you will not find a god like our God. There is no god like Him! At the centre of the cosmos there is the most perfect relationship – Father and Son bound together in selfless love by the Holy Spirit. From where we stand, that is strange, for we would never have come up with that, but hopefully you find it attractive too?

With that kind of God behind history, let's go back to the beginning and see where humans come into the story.

2 The Culmination of His Creation: The One-Flesh Couple

• GENESIS 1–2

… Remember that the dullest most uninteresting person you can talk to may one day be a creature which, if you saw it now, you would be strongly tempted to worship. … There are no ordinary people. You have never talked to a mere mortal. Nations, cultures, arts, civilizations – these are mortal, and their life is to ours as the life of a gnat. But it is immortals whom we joke with, work with, marry, snub, and exploit – immortal horrors or everlasting splendors.[1]

C. S. Lewis

---

1. C. S. Lewis, 'The Weight of Glory' in Theology, November 1941.

Why isn't this the first chapter? Should we not have started at Genesis 1? Certainly, that is where God begins, but there is also a reason why we didn't start there. It is all about assumed knowledge. The Bible begins simply, 'In the beginning God ...' Four words in and our assumed knowledge springs into action. Ah, 'God,' yes I know about Him.

The reason we had a first chapter was to undermine our confidence that we know who God is. Apart from His self-revelation we are doomed to define God as a steroid-enhanced version of our own egos. We naturally think that God is the ultimate ego, the One who is concerned with being the brightest and the strongest. And before we know it, we launch into the Bible with thousands of years of baggage in our thinking.

Everyone assumes that God is primarily concerned with demonstrating His power, thus Genesis 1 is always read as a presentation of divine power. But as we read through the Bible, is God's main concern really to prove His power? Do we read 'His impressive power and absolute authority endures forever'? No! Over and over the Bible repeats: 'His steadfast love endures forever.'

God's nature determines everything that follows. If God were a singular being, self-absorbed and eternally silent (nobody to talk to or listen to), then creation might well be a manifestation of power. (In that case, maybe creation would not have been spoken into being? Maybe it would have come after a 'flex and point'?) Without diversity within Himself, we can only guess what creation might have been like: one type of functional fish, a generic grey plant, and maybe people who were made simply to serve and obey. Life, but grey.

I mentioned Richard Sibbes in the introduction. Sibbes rejected the idea that creation is primarily about demonstrating power. 'If God had not a communicative, spreading goodness,

He would never have created the world. The Father, Son, and Holy Ghost were happy in themselves, and enjoyed one another before the world was. Apart from the fact that God delights to communicate and spread His goodness, there had never been a creation or redemption.'[2]

In the beginning God created the heavens and the earth, exactly as you might imagine based on who God is. There is multi-coloured diversity united in sweetest harmony. There are no two leaves the same, no two snowflakes alike, every nose unique, and yet all holding together as one wonderfully coherent world. It is a world of colour and noise and smells and life. As we gaze at the beauty of the ocean, or a mountain meadow, or a starry night, we can only imagine how much more exquisite it would have been pre-sin, pre-conflict and pre-death.

Genesis 1 offers a very flowing pattern of explanation. God spoke and it happened. Powerful, but also generous, abundant, lavish, extravagant, caring and tender. This was no realm of darkness to be ruled with an iron fist. It was a world of light and it was good. Even the darkness was not sinister. It had boundaries and would yield to the brilliance of morning.

Carefully and deliberately God set the stage for life to burst forth. The waters above and the waters below, purposefully separated by God's command. Land and sea were distinct and they were both good. The stage was set; now let life burst forth! First, the vegetation, the plants, the fruit trees. Poppies and lettuce, pomegranates and ivy, cherries and cauliflower, hibiscus and aster, pine and oak, orange and cherry, and on and on! It was good, but there was more!

---

2. Richard Sibbes, 'The Successful Seeker,' in *Works* vol. 6 (Edinburgh, Banner of Truth, 1973), p. 113.

God gave lights to guide and orient, to bring perspective and to shine down in their brilliance. Again, this was no functional generic light source. The vast galaxies of stars, the Milky Way, and stars no human would see for thousands of years. There is the perfection of the sun, with the earth orbiting at exactly the right distance to allow for life on earth. Then there is the cool light of the moon, such a different provision, but so perfectly suited to the needs of a creature yet to come. It was good.

God didn't create a functional fish, eight inches long, squared corners and matte grey. He spoke and the waters suddenly swarmed with living creatures, and the skies squawked with the life of every kind of winged creature. It was good and God now spoke further, blessing the creatures and urging them to enjoy the multiplication mechanism He had generously built into each one. Not exactly marriage – but creatures coming together to reproduce life, to join God in a ministry of multiplication. Each hatching angelfish and each hatching chick were completely unique, and yet never confusing the species.

The creation account is what you would expect from the God we caught a glimpse of in the last chapter. It is inherently relational, abundantly generous, and strangely selfless.

Then comes the sixth day, and yet more creatures! Will the creativity ever end? Sheep and cows, camel and yak, praying mantis and ant, T-rex and tigers and bears, oh my! What abundance! Again, God evaluated and it all came up good. But He was not finished, not yet. Everything to this point was just introduction. Now it was time for the pinnacle of creation:

Made in His Image

When we come to verse 26 we find God having a conversation within His own community. Read these next verses and ponder what it all means for us, God's last creation. What does it mean to be made in the image of God?

> 'Let us make man in our image, after our likeness. And let them have dominion over the fish of the sea and over the birds of the heavens and over the livestock and over all the earth and over every creeping thing that creeps on the earth.' So God created man in his own image, in the image of God he created him: male and female he created them. And God blessed them. And God said to them, 'Be fruitful and multiply and fill the earth and subdue it, and have dominion over the fish of the sea and over the birds of the heavens and over every living thing that moves on the earth.' (1:26-28)

What is the image of God? Is it some implicit reference to our cognitive capacities, or our ability to think in the abstract, or is it somehow something about our ability to make decisions? The text doesn't seem to point us in any of these directions.

Instead we are presented with a relational being called to rule in the same way that God had been ruling over all that He had made. So far that means no iron fist, no harsh subjugation of creation, no threat to the life of any creature.

A god who is all alone and always thinking only of himself would surely not make humanity with inbuilt diversity. Male and female? Oops, perhaps one of the two should be hidden away and treated like a lesser being. Actually, contrary to popular opinion, the God of the Bible celebrates the differences of male and female – only a God who is Trinity will honour women as well as men, equal yet different. Any other god would force conformity on both and subjugation on one.

Male and female speaks of both diversity and unity. Mankind was made in the image of God, male and female. The passage goes on to speak of God's generosity, for He had given them all the plants with their seeds, and the trees, and there was plenty of food for every other creature too. It was, indeed, very good.

Another Account?

The focus in chapter 2 is on that first couple, as it was in chapter 1, only now the camera has zoomed in considerably. We get to read of God forming the man and breathing the breath of life into him. Invigorated by the presence of the living Spirit of God, now the man was a truly living creature. God placed the man in a prepared place, a garden. This was no little English garden. This was abundantly irrigated by four rivers, and replete with massive resources, not least the Tree of Life with its wonderful fruit.

God urged the man to eat from any tree, except for one – The Tree of the Knowledge of Good and Evil. Eat there and you die. The warning was restricted and clear. The abundant provision was generous in the extreme.

Then God uttered truly alien words, 'It is not good ...' What was it about the situation that was not good from God's vantage point? It was not good for man to be alone. Immediately God set to work to fashion a helper for the man. As Adam named the creatures, he watched the pairs pass by. 'Clearly those are camels ... that's a pair of giraffes if ever I saw it ... how about we call those two ... sheep?' But the many pairs underlined God's concern: man was working alone.

It would make no sense, in a world made by a relational God who has forever lived in wonderful and glorious communion and fellowship, to make man and leave him alone, solitary, and isolated.

So God put Adam to sleep and carefully fashioned the most wonderful creature, and then He brought her to Adam. Here comes the end of the creation account, and interestingly, here comes the bride! As has happened so many times since, as he saw the love of his life, the manual labourer became a poet.

Throughout the creation account there has been a determinedly descriptive drive to the text. It has been poetic in form throughout the first chapter, but even there, the poetic form communicates fact after fact in a carefully crafted sequence. But now, at the climax of the creation account, we have the culmination of creation becoming adoringly poetic in the presence of his bride. *Bone of my bones, flesh of my flesh … roses are red, violets are blue, creation was amazing, but now look at you!* (more or less!)

The Big Theme Introduced

Introductions in books are for introducing key themes that will be developed as the book moves forward. The Bible is no different. In these first two chapters we have been introduced to themes that we should trace throughout the whole canon as we read on: God's generosity and care, powerfully demonstrated; God's word, the role of humanity as a walking, talking representation of the loving rule of God. But don't miss the theme that is introduced with the fireworks of Adam's poetry: marriage.

Male and female, united as one. Adam gets to speak the crescendo moment, with all his being going out to glorify this wonderful woman who stood before him. Then God gives a final comment:

'Therefore a man shall leave his father and his mother and hold fast to his wife, and they shall become one flesh.' (2:24)

This is the pattern for the primary human relationship. Children grow up and leave their parents in order to hold fast to their new spouse. Their unity of relationship and shared delight is made evident in their physical union. They become one flesh. Marriage is not some pragmatic institution invented by politicians for greater stability in society. Marriage is not the result of post-Fall sin. Marriage is pre-Fall, pre-sin, and actually, marriage is the goal of the whole story of creation, even of the Bible! Nothing reflects the other-centred, glory-giving, life-producing, self-sacrificing image of God's Triune relationship like a healthy human marriage.

Fast-forward several thousand years and much later in the Bible we stumble into this verse again, quoted by the Apostle Paul in reference to human marriage, but actually not. In Ephesians 5:31 he quotes Genesis 2:24, and then immediately clarifies that he is talking about a mystery now revealed – that is, that this is somehow speaking of Christ and the church. Really? Is Paul saying that from the very beginning, God's intent was not just to fill the earth with happily married couples, but that He intended to unite His Son with a bride made up of humans? We will return to Ephesians later, but yes, that is what Paul wrote.

The culmination of creation was a very happy couple. The whole symphony of creation united in harmonious wonder at the one-flesh couple, united together by the Spirit of God in Trinity-reflecting other-centred love and glory-giving adoration. They were both naked. They were not ashamed. Sadly, it didn't last long.

3   Divided!
(And It's Not My Fault!)

• GENESIS 3

The images of union with Christ, abiding in Christ, and participation in Christ present a multifaceted and wide-ranging theology of salvation. No part of human identity goes untouched by union with Christ – one's life is found in Christ, by the Spirit, in service to the Father. But much in modern theology and church life has obscured the negative corollary to union and communion, which scripture also addresses: in ourselves, we are dead, slaves, and can do 'nothing' to produce fruit.[1]

J. Todd Billings

1. J. Todd Billings, *Union with Christ: Reframing Theology and Ministry for the Church* (Grand Rapids, MI: Baker Academic, 2011), p. 11.

'That thing' (she pointed at the mirror) 'is me and not me.'

'But if you do not look you will never know how beautiful you are.'

'It comes into my mind, Stranger,' she answered, 'that a fruit does not eat itself, and a man cannot be together with himself.'

'A fruit cannot do that because it is only a fruit,' said the Un-man. 'But we can do it. We call this thing a mirror. A man can love himself, and be together with himself. That is what it means to be a man or a woman – to walk alongside oneself as if one were a second person and to delight in one's own beauty. Mirrors were made to teach this art.'[2]

C. S. LEWIS, *Perelandra*

The happy couple were more influential than they knew. Their descendants would fill the earth and live every moment of every day in a reality shaped by them, our first parents. When a marriage fails, the children always get hurt. When this couple failed, the consequences would reverberate for the rest of history.

The creation account ended on a relational high. Male and female were united in matrimony, the pinnacle of God's design. In fact, as we saw in the last chapter, God's design went way beyond Mr and Mrs Adam. God's plan was for humanity to become the bride of His Son and thereby receive so much more than would naturally be ours.

We don't know how long they lived before chapter three. The fact that they did not have children under perfect

---

2. C. S. Lewis, *Perelandra* (1944, Scribner Classics Edition, 1996), p. 117.

conditions for conception implies it was a relatively short season of innocence – knowing good, but not evil. The next thing we see is Eve in a conversation with a crafty serpent in the garden. The conversation that ensues is like peeling the layers of an onion, and it should make you cry! Before we continue, let's ponder where this serpent came from.

Mirror Mirror on the Wall!

Ezekiel gives us the explanation of how the enemy ended up being the great antagonist of all that is godly and good. In the middle section of his prophecy, Ezekiel offers a series of burdens against the nations around Judah. In chapter twenty-eight he launches a verbal prophetic assault against the prince of Tyre.

Here was a man who acted like he was a god. Like many national rulers down through the years, he had got carried away with his power and crossed the line from pride into blasphemy. He thought he knew it all, and through the prophet, God made it clear what He thought of him. His pride in his power and position was profoundly problematic from God's perspective. So God determined to bring foreigners against him to destroy him.

Yet it seems that the prince of Tyre, for all his grandiose claims, was something of a puppet. Behind him was the King of Tyre – a figure of far greater historic proportions. From verse eleven to nineteen we get to read of the Satanic figure behind the puppet prince. Who would prompt a human to presume devilish divinity?

This being was no mere human. He was the 'signet of perfection, full of wisdom and perfect in beauty.' Furthermore, he was 'in Eden, the garden of God.' He was covered with every precious stone – a uniform for reflecting glory, for this was an anointed guardian cherub. This being was perfect, until unrighteousness was found in him and he was cast away from God's heavenly mountain.

Why did this all happen? Why did the top angel, with the best job, suddenly go rogue? Verse seventeen tells us, 'Your heart was proud because of your beauty; you corrupted your wisdom for the sake of your splendour.' The covering cherub, one of the angels closest to the glorious centre-piece of heaven, looked at himself and pride took charge. Instead of reflecting the glorious love of God for His Son, this one was corrupted at the heart with jealousy – surely he could be glorious too?

Before we return to Eden, is it right to suggest that the covering cherub grew jealous of glorious love? Shouldn't it simply be seen as jealousy of God's glory and power? While this text does not point explicitly to the Trinitarian love and mutual delight, the ensuing rage of the enemy throughout history is not simply against God's position; it also seems to be against God's devotion. The enemy consistently despises God's Son, and anything that would promote human devotion to God. The enemy so hates the loving nature of God that he has consistently pushed a corrupted view of God, a view low on love and high on power – the kind of 'god-like-ness' that was offered in the Garden of Eden, and the kind seen in the prince of Tyre, his charge in this passage. (Incidentally, we see the same manifestations in the human king of Babylon in Isaiah fourteen – devilish pseudo-divinity indeed!)

So back to the earthly Eden:

The War of the Words

The serpent launched his attack with scepticism. 'Did God actually say ...?' Eve had no reason to distrust God's words. At the same time, she was the more vulnerable of the two humans since she had apparently heard the instruction via her husband. Perhaps Adam had misunderstood? Perhaps God actually shouldn't be trusted? What if God was holding something back from this naïve pair of human beings?

Eve's eager clarification that they could eat from any tree, but not the fruit of the tree in the midst of the garden inadvertently played right into the hands (as it were) of the serpent. By his tricky question about all the trees, Eve was now looking at the one particular tree she shouldn't be dwelling on. This was the tree that Adam had explained to her, 'Listen, dear, let's not go anywhere near that – God said we'd die if we eat, so let's not even touch, okay?!' Now she was drawn into conversation about it and about God's trustworthiness. She was set up for The Lie. And here begins the ages long war of the words – will we trust God's word, or the serpent's? Most people go with the serpent's words:

> 'You will not surely die. For God knows that when you eat of it your eyes will be opened, and you will be like God, knowing good and evil.' (Gen. 3:4-5)

The Lie

The Lie is not as simple as it looks. In fact, we must not treat it as a simple singular lie. This is like peeling the layers of an onion. Let's start with the obvious one and start peeling.

1. ***You will be like God***. God is God and we are not. That is clear. Her response should have been to interrupt and beg to differ, 'No we won't!' Or should it have been? Actually, if Eve had been doing her quiet time in Genesis 1 and 2, then she should have had another answer. 'Firstly, Mr Snake, I already am like God! My husband and I were made in His image. And secondly,

the 'god' you are telling me I can be like is not like the God I know!'

2. **Which God?** The 'god' that the serpent was offering to Eve was entirely different from the relational and generous glory-giving God of creation. The serpent was suggesting that to be like god was to be autonomous, self-concerned, creatively a-moral. The offer with a hiss was a multi-layered lie, even about God Himself. The offer was to be a rival god, an autonomous and a-relational self-referential god. Eve was being offered the opportunity to be like Satan, the god of this age, not like the true creator God.

3. **You will not die.** God had said that in the day they ate of that tree, they would die. Did they? Here was a speaking, thinking, moving being who obviously knew there was something beyond the bite and he didn't seem to be dead. Besides, they didn't die physically for years. They did *begin* to die physically. But did they actually die that day? In John 3 Jesus spoke to religious expert Nicodemus who clearly assumed he was already alive. However, Jesus refused to engage in his conversation about the kingdom of God because Nicodemus needed to be born of the Spirit. When Adam and Eve bit the bait of The Lie, they died instantly. Why? Because they lost the Spirit who bonded them to each other and to God. Suddenly each relationship was a threat, instead of being life-giving. We will see evidence of this soon.

4. **Eyes opened, you will be like God, knowing good and evil.** Here is another layer of The Lie. The hissing

version of god implied the potential for power through knowledge. That is, Adam and Eve would be able to also know good and evil but remain uncorrupted by it. God is all-knowing and unmarred by sin. We would do well to learn that we don't have that capacity. The knowledge of evil corrupts us more than we will ever admit. In a world that mocks innocence, perhaps we too have bought into this lie too much when we pursue 'mature awareness' of things best left alone.

And so The Lie took hold. She looked. She wanted. She desired. She bit.

Tradition tells us the fruit was an apple. That seems a bit unfair to apples! Perhaps it was a cherry (or perhaps that is my lingering dislike of the flavour from cough medicine received as a child!) It probably was not a lemon though. How can we know that? Because the 'lemon' was standing there with her and saying nothing! Adam was *with* her. Oh, what a shameful moment. She was deceived and entangled in the conversation, but he went in eyes wide open. When a serpent engages your wife, you fetch a broom and get rid of it. Adam didn't.

Before we leave The Lie, let me point out that there are four occasions in the New Testament where The Lie is mentioned. Typically it is translated as 'lies' or 'falsehood', but literally it should be 'The Lie.' For example, in John 8 Jesus is talking with some Jews who claim God is their father, but Jesus points out that their father is the devil (not a great PR moment in Jesus' ministry, but very enlightening!) They might claim God as their father, but if He were, then they would love Jesus. Instead, Jesus says, they shared the desires of the devil – a murderer from the beginning, one who does not stand in <u>the truth</u>, because there is no truth in him. 'When he speaks <u>the lie</u>, he speaks out of his own character for he is a liar and the father of <u>it</u>' (literal translation of John 8:44 – see also Romans 1:25; Ephesians 4:25, 2 Thessalonians 2:11).

Relational Collapse and Fig-Leaves

The serpent's offer was a poor one. They already had knowledge of good, but now they added an intimate and destructive engagement with evil. They thought they would become God-like, but instead they gained awareness of their nakedness. Actually, this *was* god-likeness – god of this age-likeness. Now humanity was spiritually dead, relationally corrupted and curved in on their own pathetic universe where self is a god desperately grasping at glory despite its deadness.

Immediately they started to 'fig-leaf' – to pretend that they weren't naked and inadequate, to pretend they were alive and somebody special, when in fact they were dead already. We have all been 'fig-leafing' our way through life ever since.

What is more, the loss of the Spirit is immediately evident in their relationships. They hid from God and they started blaming and competing with each other. The gardener-poet who adored his lovely wife now grudgingly lived with the woman he needed, but his concern was more for covering his own nakedness than engaging in true relational union with her.

God did not want them walking around in the myth of their godlike status covered by fig leaves. He wanted them to know they were dead, and that their sin meant death. It is impossible to imagine the shock as they saw that first animal slaughtered to give them a hideous pair of his and hers fur coats still dripping with blood.

The Marriage Plan Shattered?

The Fall of Genesis 3 has made every marriage profoundly difficult. As God spoke to the man and woman He laid out some of the implications. The ground was now cursed and so man would find work incredibly difficult from then on. The woman would also find life difficult, both in her relationship with Mr Lemon, who she would now want to rule over, and in giving birth to children, which would now surpass any labour they could ever have imagined. They would also be banished from the garden, for God would not want these spiritual zombies accessing the Tree of Life and living forever in this state of death. But there was good news. The serpent was cursed, and God had a plan to undo the dark magic of Genesis 3. God would crush the head of the serpent through the seed of the woman! There was yet hope for humanity, and therefore, hope for humanity and God to be in relationship!

4 **Of Wells and Wives**

• GENESIS

It is true, a child may sometimes marry against his father's consent, one whom he may be ashamed to bring to his father's house, because she will disgrace it; but how mean and sinful soever we are in ourselves, when once we are betrothed to Christ, he will not think it any dishonor to acknowledge us even before his Father, but account it his glory, before him and blessed angels, that he has such a spouse.[1]

JEREMIAH BURROUGHS

But, where this rich and loving husband, Christ, takes unto wife this poor and wicked Harlot, redeeming her from all

---

1. Jeremiah Burroughs, *An Exposition of Hosea* (Edinburgh: James Nichol, 1863), p. 160.

evils, laying all her sins upon his own shoulders; whereby they are swallowed up in him, as darkness is swallowed up in the Sun-beams. For it behooves that all sin be swallowed up at the very sight of Christ, clothing and enrobing her with his own righteousness, and garnishing her with all his own Jewels. Whose hearts, hearing these things, will not melt for very joy, and wax ravished for very love of Christ, having received so great consolation? [2]

JOHN EATON

Sin's impact on human relationships did not take long to manifest. The first siblings were the first murderer and his victim. In fact, as we read through Genesis it seems like generally depressing reading. People were trying to make a name for themselves, but failing to care for each other. And in the midst of it all, there is a persistently faithful God working out His promise to deal with sin through the seed of the woman.

The line of promise is fairly easy to trace through Genesis. After a subtle hint about Shem in Genesis 9:27, we then see Abram come into focus as the one in whose line the seed and the blessing will come (Gen. 12:1-3, 7; 22:17-18). Next is Abram's second-born son Isaac (Gen. 26:2-3), then his second-born son Jacob (Gen. 28:13-15; 32:29), and then his fourth-born son, Judah (Gen. 49:10 – the language here is of the coming ruler).

What is astonishing is how messed up these families were! The Patriarchs did not float twelve inches above the ground and wear halos. Genesis is no stained glass window.

---

2. John Eaton, *The Honey-Combe of Free Justification* (London, 1642, edited by Robert Lancaster), p. 465.

Abraham's Lingering Issue

Abraham is called the great father of faith. That could be misleading. His faith faltered and flickered and fumbled along. He seemed to obey God, kind of. God called him to leave his birth family and head to the Promised Land. Instead he took his family and went halfway there. Once his father died, he travelled on, but kept his nephew with him. He got to the Promised Land, and overshot; he landed in Egypt and promptly gave his wife away. God protected Sarai; Abraham didn't. Great father of faith-*ish*.

When Abram did separate from Lot, God reaffirmed His plan to bless his seed with the land. When he rescued some kings and was offered payment, Abram declared his reliance on God. It was after this that Abram believed God's Word and it was credited to him as righteousness (Gen.15:6). God promptly reinforced the great promise with a stunning covenantal ceremony. The ceremony made it clear that God's plan depended only on God for fulfilment.

What we find in the Bible is that God is more inclined to give a covenant bordering on a testament, than one akin to a mercantile contract. There is a difference. Testament-type covenants tend to be more one-sided and dependent on God's faithfulness to the promise of His grace. Contracts tend to involve performance and reward, creating a very different relationship between parties. Marriage, our great theme, is a permanent and secure covenant, not a performance-based contract. We must keep that in mind as we go through the Bible and think about God's relationship with humanity.

Next thing we know, Abraham is taking heat from Sarai who has come up with a plan to 'fig-leaf' her barrenness. Even though Sarai was the one who suggested that Abram lie with her Egyptian maidservant, going outside the marital bond never bodes well. Sure enough, tension ensued between Sarai and Abram, and between Sarai and Hagar. (Yet God faithfully cared for the poor Egyptian and her son.)

Abraham had a wife, and God intended to honour that reality, even if Abraham didn't. Sarah (new name) would give birth to 'little-boy-laughter', a name that made sense not only because of the joy of his birth, but also after both parents laughed at the suggestion of his birth! Combine the specific promise of Isaac's birth with the visit of the LORD in chapter 18, followed by the destruction of Sodom, and you have to scratch your head at what happens in chapter 20. Abraham then gives his wife away, again! And again, God protected her where her husband didn't. The man of faith? Sort of.

The high point of the story follows with Abraham obediently taking Isaac to Mt Moriah for a heartbreaking sacrifice. Finally he trusts God and it all ends well. Actually, as Sarah dies, Abraham starts to make moves to find a bride for his son.

Isaac's Bride: All is not Well

Abraham was now, finally, a man of faith. He trusted that God would provide the right wife for Isaac – a woman from their extended family (and also outside of Canaanite territory!). So he sent his servant off with gifts in tow, to find the bride. He met her at a well. Wells seemed to be the place to go in those days. Sure enough, an attractive and generous unmarried relative showed up, water was drawn, a meal invitation given, and the marriage was arranged. Isaac may be the passive Patriarch, but Rebekah is always presented in a flurry of action. Indeed, Rebekah was impressive, but it was God's steadfast love and faithfulness in helping the servant to find her that was celebrated (see Gen. 24:27). Rebekah was coming back to be Mrs Isaac. With Sarah now gone, a new lady would be on centre stage.

Isaac and Rebekah seemed to be a happy couple, but once their 'different as chalk and cheese' twin boys were born, we find the first hint of division in the marriage (Gen. 25:28). Just like his father, Isaac tried to give his wife away! Two generations and three times in less than fifteen chapters? Something must be broken in human marriage!

As the story moves on, we find Rebekah working against Isaac to facilitate the rise of her preferred son, Jacob. Her kitchen conspiracy created massive family meltdown and Jacob had to flee for his life.

As Jacob heads away to find his bride, we also get a glimpse of Esau choosing to marry a daughter of Ishmael. The irony is that the unchosen son marries one from the line of another unchosen son. Marrying someone from the wrong line, or the wrong race, really mattered in the Old Testament. It was not a matter of racism, but of devotion to God and His covenant, and avoiding the danger of misdirected devotion.

Jacob's Brides: Well, Not So Well

What happens when an immovable object meets an irresistible force? Jacob, meet Laban. Jacob was the trickiest of characters. He got things for himself in his own way. Laban was equally tricky. Their years together became a great game of chess. It all started well, at a well. It was noon and Rachel showed up with her sheep. Jacob practically proposed on the spot! Actually, the well may have been the place to find a bride, but Jacob had to work for his beloved. There was a large stone serving as an obstacle, but Jacob wrestled it out of the way.

Jacob's need to work for his wife continued as Laban tricked him into first marrying Leah, the elder daughter. Jacob worked for years and ended up with a truly complex family. The wife he did not want gave him his first four boys. Then Rachel, his beloved, gave him her servant who gave him two more boys. Leah retaliated with her servant, add another two. Leah then had another two boys, plus a girl. Finally, beloved Rachel bore Jacob a son: Joseph. Jacob had been his mother's favourite. Now his favourite wife gave him a son, who naturally became his favourite. It is not hard to imagine the tensions that would follow from such a blended and complex family!

Jacob finally broke free from Laban and headed back toward the Promised Land. When he had crossed the border during his hasty departure he had received a stunning vision of the stairway connecting heaven and earth, as well as a reiteration that God's promise applied to him despite everything he had done. Now as he approached the border he might well have anticipated another heavenly encounter.

Jacob was still a self-serving and manipulative character. In Genesis 32 we see him preparing for the fearful reunion with his angry brother Esau. He sent group after group of gifts to his brother. He even sent wives and children ahead of himself. His reasoning was simple. 'If Esau attacks, at least I can survive.' This all changes by Genesis 33.

Jacob spent a night alone after he had sent his wives and children ahead of him. Suddenly he found himself wrestling with a man in the night. The wrestler had incredible powers, but Jacob was persistent and would not let go until he received some sort of blessing. Maybe he thought this was an angel and he must get something out of him. Eventually Jacob asked for the man's name and the response stirred great awe in him – afterwards he named the place Peniel, because he had 'seen the face of God and lived'.

Jacob learned a lesson we all need to learn. His biggest issue was not Esau, or Laban, or any other circumstance. His biggest issue was his view of God. He didn't believe that he could trust God's Word, but instead felt like he had to control his own life and circumstances. We all have a little bit of Jacob in us – an inclination to manipulate and control circumstances. Next thing we read is Jacob leading the way, before his wives and children, to go and meet Esau.

Jacob's family life remained complex. His firstborn, Reuben, lost all credibility by defiling his father's marital bed. His next two, Simeon and Levi, were always creating trouble. When their sister Dinah was shamed by Shechem, these two concocted a deceptive circumcision and destruction plot that left Jacob fuming as the whole land would now have a low view of their family. Then there was the fourth son, Judah.

We tend to think of the last chapters of Genesis being all about Joseph. In many ways he is the focus of the text as he was the focus of Jacob's affections. We need the story of Joseph to understand how the family ended up in Egypt and turned into a nation there before Exodus could be written. But there is another purpose for the story of Joseph: it serves as a backdrop to show the development of Judah.

Judah is the fourth Patriarch in the line of the Messiah. Like the three generations before him, his life is marked by marital complexities. Genesis 38 is one of those chapters that causes people to scratch their heads. Why interrupt the story of Joseph for the mess of Judah? Joseph was leaving the land as a captive, but Judah left voluntarily. Joseph's 'death' was really that of a goat; Judah offered a goat in payment for inadvertently giving life. Joseph's coat had been used to deceive his father, but Judah was deceived by a woman in fancy dress. Actually, Joseph ended up leaving his garment behind to escape the wiles of Mrs Potiphar, but Judah was caught out by what he left behind. (Compare Joseph's story in Genesis 37 and 39 with Judah in Genesis 38.)

Judah married a foreigner, and she turned out to be more righteous than him. Tamar was left without children and Judah did not allow his third son to marry her as was required by the Law. So she took matters into her own hands. She deceived Judah and got pregnant by him. Judah is not impressive in Genesis 38, but he is responsive. By the end of the chapter he acknowledges her superior righteousness.

Fast forward some years and Judah is the one brother who is willing to lay down his life for his father's precious son. As unrecognised Joseph played chess with his brothers, Reuben had offered Jacob the nonsensical security of being able to kill grandsons if his precious son was not brought back safely from Egypt. But Judah is the one who finally steps in and sets Benjamin free so that Jacob not only keeps his precious son, but is then reunited to the long-lost older brother, Joseph. Maybe the story of Joseph is really the backdrop for the development of the character of Judah?

Another Well

As we move out of Genesis we find the next big character making marital arrangements at a well. In Exodus 2 Moses fled to Midian after killing an Egyptian who was mistreating an Israelite. There we find him at a well as he finds his foreign wife. For Moses the brief scene involves fighting some antagonistic shepherds, drawing out the water and caring for a flock. It was ironic really, since Moses was himself drawn out of water, he would lead his people through the water and had decades of conflict ahead of him as he would shepherd God's flock. We will ponder Moses and the people of Israel more in the next chapter as the marital themes continue to develop.

Foreign Wells and the Worst of Wives

Many generations later, another Jew stopped at a foreign well in the heat of the day. It was Jacob's well. A woman also came to the well and soon found herself in a conversation with this Jew as He rested there. The very fact that they were conversing was scandalous, but that did not surprise her. Many men had engaged her in conversation that inevitably seemed to lead to shared phone numbers and heartache. What surprised her on this occasion was the ethnicity issue – He was a Jew, she was a Samaritan.

There was almost nowhere lower on the totem pole than to be a Samaritan woman. Actually, she had gone lower. She had lived a dubious life and the women of the town treated her as an outcast – perhaps none felt their husbands were safe with this woman around. So she endured trips to the well in the noontime sun to avoid the heat of their comments. Here was a woman who had somehow been married five times (Hollywood divorce rate or poor cooking, either way it was not good), and the man she was living with was not her husband.

So this foreigner engaged her with the strangest pick-up line. After asking for water, He started saying she should have asked Him for living water that bubbles up within and satisfies forever. She didn't know who He was.

Next thing she knew, this man who seemed to be trying to connect illicitly starts talking about her 'husband' – and He knew her history! The stranger had gone from 'a Jew' to 'sir' and now, 'a prophet'. Since the man knew an uncomfortable amount of information about her home life, she decided to engage Him in a discussion about religion. No problem, this man could hold a conversation about religion and He proceeded to reinforce the fact that God desired true spirit-filled worshippers.

Finally there comes one of the most beautiful moments in the Bible. This nobody with a terrible reputation raised the issue of the Messiah, and Jesus graciously and freely introduced Himself – 'I am!' (John 4:26). After excusing herself from the awkwardness of twelve staring men elbowing each other, this woman was transformed, rushing into the town and stirring up the harvest of people to flock to Jesus, the Messiah, who they would discover to be the saviour of the world!

The creation account culminated with man and wife coming together. This is God's plan. He will not merely rescue humanity from the mess we've made, but in the process, God's intention is to call out a bride for His Son … a bride of nobodies, of sinful nobodies, of foreign sinful nobodies. Watch Jesus at the well: with perfect tenderness He woos His bride.

5 The Jealous God

• EXODUS 19, 32

God is the highest good of the reasonable creature. The enjoyment of him is our proper happiness, and is the only happiness with which our souls can be satisfied. To go to heaven, fully to enjoy God, is infinitely better than the most pleasant accommodations here: better than fathers and mothers, husbands, wives, or children, or the company of any or all earthly friends. These are but shadows; but God is the substance. These are but scattered beams; but God is the sun. These are but streams; but God is the fountain. These are but drops; but God is the ocean. Therefore, it becomes us to spend this life only as a journey towards heaven.[1]

JONATHAN EDWARDS

---

1. Jonathan Edwards, 'The True Christian's Life a Journey Towards Heaven,' *WJE* 17: 437-38, cited in Dane Ortlund's *Edwards on the Christian Life*, Crossway, 2014, p. 132.

The God of Genesis is a God who repeatedly makes promises to several generations of one family and then plants them in Egypt. Between Genesis and Exodus that family in Egypt grows into a nation. The God of Exodus is a God who births a nation out of Egypt to make them His family.

The Bible has some blank pages. Perhaps the most famous comes between the Old and New Testament – over 400 years of some of the most intense and fascinating history, changes of world empires, political turmoil, etc., all covered by a blank page. Another critical blank page comes between Genesis and Exodus – over 400 years of transition from favoured family to persecuted people in the kiln that was Egypt. It is hard for us to fathom how God could, by inspiration, jump four hundred years of history. However, we can trust that God's view is much bigger than ours and He selected what was right to include in the history of the Bible.

So as Exodus begins, Israel has become a nation now considered a threat to the changing powers-that-be in Egypt. We are quickly introduced to Moses, a man divinely protected and given the best of education for national leadership: in the privileged schools of Egypt, and the shepherding school of hard knocks in Midian. One day, shepherd Moses saw the Angel of the LORD in a bush that was burning, but not burning up. He met the LORD. God identified Himself as the God of Abraham, Isaac and Jacob, and then spoke of how He had seen the affliction of 'my people' and planned to deliver them. Here is the God of Genesis promising to follow through with Exodus deliverance.

The Covenant God

As the tension rises between Moses and Pharaoh, God makes it clear to Moses who is in charge. Pharaoh will drive them out of his land, but God will be behind it. In the first verses of chapter 6, God underlines His commitments – He had appeared to Abraham, Isaac and Jacob, but now He was making Himself known by name to Moses. He had promised the earlier Patriarchs the land, but now He was responding to the groans of the people and was ready to remember His covenant with them.

It must be awesome to hear that the God who made everything intends to deliver you from slavery, redeeming you with an outstretched arm and great acts of judgment. But the relational connection quotient is multiplied in the next verse (6:7). 'I will take you to be my people, and I will be your God, and you shall know that I am the LORD your God, who has brought you out from under the burdens of the Egyptians.' Well, it would be awesome, if you believed the message, but the Israelites did not. God fulfilled His promise anyway.

Pharaoh hardened his heart against Moses, and God cemented that determination as the pressures increased. Pharaoh's magicians could not keep up their copycat charade, then ten plagues later Pharaoh was a broken man and Israel was released. As the Israelites saw the Egyptians dead on the shores of the Red Sea, they feared the LORD and they believed in Him and His servant, Moses (see 14:31).

Moses sang a song to celebrate (Exod. 15:1-18). He sang of God's glorious power over their enemies. He sang of God's steadfast love toward His people. This was their God, and these were His people.

The Marital Ceremony?

When we come to Exodus 19 we stumble upon a scene with marital ideas floating in the air. God has brought the people of Israel to Himself and now they have the opportunity to become God's treasured possession among all the peoples, a kingdom of priests and a holy nation. In the early verses, God declares His intention!

In verse 8 we have the people declaring their willingness to go along with God's plan. God tells Moses to get the people consecrated and to prepare their garments for the third day, when the Lord will come down to them in their sight. They are to stay back from the mountain until the trumpet blast signals the time to approach. This is a time of preparation and separation in anticipation of the coming wedding celebration.

So on the third day, we read that Moses brought the people out to meet God (19:17). This was an intense moment. Here God is presented in all His power, majesty, purity and splendour.

At this time God gave them the Ten Commandments, but the people pulled back in fear and did not want to deal with God directly. After a few short chapters of covenant guidelines, we find the covenant being confirmed in Exodus 24. Moses read the book of the covenant, and the people declared their commitment to God. Moses sprinkled the people with blood to confirm the binding covenant. The representative leaders of the nation were with Moses and they saw God. (This was surely God the Son, since nobody gets to see the Father. It is always the Son who reveals the Father to humanity.)

As Moses was up on the mountain with God, there are two things to note. First, God reiterated the marital content of the covenant between Him and the people. In Exodus 29:45-46 we read that God will dwell with Israel and be their God. He is committed. Second, they weren't ...

Spiritual Adultery and a Jealous Husband!

While Moses was still on the mountain with God, the people of Israel were already whoring after other lovers. If Exodus 19 had some wedding themes in it, the books of Moses as a whole ring with the shocking themes of human infidelity, whoredom and the failure of the covenant of Sinai. (Actually, the books of Moses as a whole point beyond the failure of the Sinai covenant to the hope of a future 'by faith' covenant that would be enacted by the coming King for His kingdom … more on that soon!)

It seems truly bizarre that the people of Israel would so quickly desert the God who loved them so much. Actually, adultery is usually bizarre and senseless. God had rescued them from Egypt and cared for them in the wilderness. He had made wonderful promises to them and demonstrated His own great power (i.e. He could follow through on what He said). But they grew impatient after a few days and had Aaron make another god for them.

The god they wanted was fashioned after fallen thinking. They wanted a god that looked impressive and powerful, so they got a bull-calf made of gold. This was an image of strength and power; it was impressive, at least within the fantasy they were pursuing in their flight from their faithful God. Actually, the true God is more powerful, but perhaps less obsessed with His own power. So, calling this stand-in lover 'the LORD', they let loose and lived the party lifestyle together in front of it.

The true God was not unaware, of course, and He sent Moses down, commenting on how quickly these people had failed and gone astray. God, as any jilted husband would be, was furious!

Moses headed down toward the camp. Joshua was with him and mistook the noise for a victory celebration after a battle. Moses knew it wasn't that, nor the noise of defeat. This was the noise of a people letting loose and dropping all their inhibitions. When Moses got closer, he was crystal clear as to God's perspective on the drunken insanity. Quickly the false god was destroyed and Moses forced it down their throats before turning to his brother Aaron for an explanation.

If the situation were not so serious, Aaron's response would be laughable. Unable to offer a convincing lie, he went for the old classic – 'it just happened on its own!' Children down through the centuries, not to mention some scientists, have resorted to this explanation for things when the truth would be problematic, but no better explanation comes to mind.

This moment was critical for Israel. The nation birthed and made to be a kingdom of priests had corrupted their calling. Now Moses called out the faithful and the tribe of Levi had their first priestly duty – a sacrifice for sin of horrendous proportions. Three thousand men fell by the sword.

The Glory of the Jealous God

The next day Moses headed back up the mountain. He was ready to speak for the people to their God. This was crisis marital intervention, for truly this marriage was absolutely on the rocks. They had been grossly unfaithful, and their perfect husband was righteously indignant.

Moses went to God on behalf of His people. Moses asked God to condemn him and spare the nation. Many years later God Himself would do something similar – sacrifice Himself so undeserving sinners could be saved.

As we enter chapter 33, God has relented of destroying the people. He is willing to give them what they don't deserve – the land, the blessings, etc. He even offers an angel for their protection, but He refuses to go with them lest His holy presence destroy these sinners.

This intense conversation between Moses and the LORD keeps going in the text, but Exodus offers us an intriguing and explanatory interlude at this point. The text explains how Moses was in the habit of going to meet the LORD in the tent of meeting. We read that Moses and the LORD would 'speak face to face, as a man speaks to his friend'. Really? Why is this information here? Because of what came next in the crisis conversation.

Moses seems to be growing in boldness as he speaks with the LORD on the mountain. He identifies the nation as 'your people' and gets God to agree to go with them. Suddenly Moses pushes the boat out a little too far for comfort. Here he is on the mountain with a legitimately angry betrayed husband who is all-powerful. Any sane man in this situation would be looking for the end of the conversation and the way out. But not Moses; instead of asking to see the exit, he asks to see the LORD's glory!

This is a perplexing and thrilling moment in the unfolding story of God and His people. Moses has the confidence to request a viewing of the LORD's glory (I believe, because He already knew the LORD down in the tent). We might anticipate a power display to frighten the sandal-socks off every person within fifty miles, especially when God makes it clear that nobody can see His face and live (which feels like a contradiction to the face-to-face meetings in the tent).

The LORD high up on the mountain, whose face nobody can see, is willing to show Moses His glory. Moses believed it was worth asking in light of his own face-to-face encounters with the LORD in the tent down near the people ... perhaps the LORD who comes to the tent near the people somehow reveals the LORD who is high on the mountain and nobody can see? (See John 1:14-18 to see this explained in some detail.)

But we still haven't noticed the shocking display of God's glory to Moses. This is not the ultimate power demonstration we might expect. Instead God says, 'I will make all my goodness pass before you and will proclaim before you my name "The LORD". And I will be gracious to whom I will be gracious, and will show mercy on whom I will show mercy.' I wasn't expecting that. It seems that Moses was, though.

In chapter 34 we read of the actual glory display. These verses become the most quoted Old Testament text in the Old Testament. This is not just for Moses' benefit, for God tells him to bring two stone tablets (is God really going to pursue the marriage relationship after what they did?) Imagine being there for this:

> The LORD descended in the cloud and stood with him there, and proclaimed the name of the LORD. The LORD passed before him and proclaimed, 'The LORD, the LORD, a God merciful and gracious, slow to anger, and abounding in steadfast love and faithfulness, keeping steadfast love for thousands, forgiving iniquity and transgression and sin, but who will by no means clear the guilty, visiting the iniquity of the fathers on the children and the children's children, to the third and the fourth generation.' (Exod. 34:5-7)

The glory of this God is so shockingly good that surely our response should be the same as that of Moses. Let us bow our heads and worship! The glory of the LORD is His mercy, grace, slowness to anger, His loyalty and forgiveness, and abundant steadfast love and faithfulness (in John 1:15 this would be rendered, 'full of grace and truth!'). And at the end, just to be clear, this is no wishy-washy God of sappy niceness, for He takes sin very seriously and will deal with it justly!

In light of the gloriously loving and self-giving character of the LORD, Moses then ties together his bizarre request with the flow of the conversation before that. 'In light of that, LORD, go with us, forgive us, make us your inheritance.' Those are marital words, Moses! And God said? I do.

Covenant Renewed

Actually, God said, 'Behold, I am making a covenant.' He goes on to detail what He will do in their midst, what He will do before them. God calls on the people to be faithful and loyal, to avoid any flirting with the idols of the nations that stand before them, any whoring after those nothing gods, because God's name is Jealous! God's speech in Exodus 34 calls for loyalty and distance from any metal mini-god that will draw their hearts, or their children's hearts, away from devotion to Him.

When Moses finally returned to the people, his face shone with the glory of God. Getting close to God left a lingering effect. Years later the apostle Paul would describe how that glory faded and needed to be covered by a veil; but now we are able, by union with Christ through the Spirit, to look on the glory of the Lord and continue to be transformed without the need for any sort of veil. For us the glory gives way to more glory. Something greater must be true today than was true for Moses. The story of God's relating to humanity gets richer the further we read through the Bible!

6 The Bible's Biggest Big Idea

• LEVITICUS 26:11-12 (traced through Bible)

When the bridegroom has the bride's heart, it is a right marriage: but some give their hand to Christ, who do not give their heart. Those who are only driven to Christ by terror, will surely leave him again when that terror is gone. Terror may break a heart of stone – but the pieces into which it is broken still continue to be stone; terrors cannot soften it into a heart of flesh. Yet terrors may begin the work which love crowns. The strong wind, and the earthquake, and the fire going before; the still small voice, in which the Lord is, may come after them.

As soon as the believer is united to Christ, Christ himself, in whom all fullness dwells, is his, Cant. 2:16, 'My beloved is mine, and I am his.' And 'how shall he not with him freely give us all things?' Romans 8:32.[1]

THOMAS BOSTON

Heaven is a place of supreme beauty. It is a place of infinite happiness. This happiness is the joy of the Father and the Son delighting in one another. There we are with Christ in open fellowship, as his own bride. Christ exudes a light and a brightness. We participate in Christ's own glory and happiness. This joy is expressed in glad praise – Edwards says many times throughout his writings that the chief joy of heaven will be that we will finally be able to *express* our love to God. All this will never end.[2]

DANE ORTLUND

God's intention was to have a special people of His own. He would be their God and they would be His people. He had declared this in anticipation of Sinai in Exodus 6, then restated it again at the establishment of the covenant in Exodus 29. God wanted to dwell in the midst of His people. So He led them to Sinai and brought them into covenant with Him. The guidelines that came with the covenant were fairly straightforward, but within a few chapters disaster had put the marriage covenant immediately under question.

God's gift to His people was Himself. But when they sinned, He added law. And since they sinned a lot, He added lots of law. It is easy to think of the Law of Moses as a great block of instructions dropped from the throne of heaven on

---

1. Thomas Boston, *Human Nature in Its Four Fold State* (Bungay, 1812), p. 252.
2. Dane Ortlund, *Edwards on the Christian Life: Alive to the Beauty of God* (Wheaton, IL: Crossway, 2014), p. 169.

to the people of Israel. Actually, the Law develops and grows. Initially, for example, they were to use a simple earthen altar. Mix in the faithlessness of the people at Sinai, the golden calf, etc., and then we find the complex priestly code running through the rest of Exodus and into Leviticus. Tabernacle, sacrifices, and offerings.

God's call on the nation was that they should be holy, devoted, settled in their adoration of Him rather than any ridiculous crawling creature that might distract their devotion. God's desire was clear, 'I am the LORD who brought you up out of the land of Egypt to be your God.' (Lev. 11:44-45) This section comes to a strong climax with the instructions for the Day of Atonement in Leviticus 16.

Then they do it again. It is so brief we can easily miss it. Leviticus 17:7 notes, almost in passing, another horrendous incident of spiritual adultery, which in turn leads to another block of laws. God stated, 'So they shall no more sacrifice their sacrifices to goat demons, after whom they whore.' God's people repeatedly played the harlot, they whored after creatures rather than the Creator. And so God had to add the final block of laws to govern the people. The kingdom of priests had gone after a bull. Now the people who had not wanted to be priests were going after goats. Bizarre. Adultery usually is.

One of the great themes of the Bible that should cause us to sit down and shake our heads in wonder, is that when God's people are unfaithful to the God who has done so much for them, He doesn't just wipe them out. In the midst of this section God reiterates again: 'I am the LORD who sanctifies you, who brought you out of the land of Egypt to be your God.' (Lev. 22:31-33; 25:38) I suspect you and I would press the wipe out button, but thankfully we are not God. After another block of law is complete, God closes the section with another restatement of the covenant. He has said it before, and now He says it again.

In Leviticus 26 God calls the people not to go after idols, but to honour Him. He promises the best of blessings if they will just remain loyal to Him. He will confirm His covenant with them. In fact, He has said it before, but now He says it again, the biggest big idea of the whole Bible, perhaps? 'I will make my dwelling among you, and my soul shall not abhor you. And I will walk among you and will be your God, and you shall be my people.' (26:11-12)

The Bible's Biggest Big Idea?

Let's take a quick jog through the Bible. It will help us see that the idea of God and His people being bound together in a loving covenantal relationship is a resounding theme. Actually, the more we see how one-sided this relationship is, the more it should break our hearts for our tendencies toward unfaithfulness, and stir our hearts with love for God because of His loyal love. This chapter will be a quick sweep through the rest of the Old Testament, looking at the theme of God's amazing faithfulness in response to the unfaithfulness of His people. Then in our next chapter, we begin part 2 which will be a more in-depth study of this theme through the Old Testament.

The God of the Bible is primarily a covenant-making and covenant-keeping God, rather than a contract God. In a contract everything is *quid pro quo* – you do this, then I'll do that. While the covenant with Israel has many *quid pro quo* features, this is not the case with God's covenant with Abraham, with David, or the New Covenant. God's great covenants are built on the solid foundation of two little words: 'I will.' When cultures turn the marriage covenant into a contract, then the institution of marriage starts to collapse. When we turn the covenant God of the Bible into a contract God, then the great marriage starts to change in tone and our understanding of the Bible starts to collapse.

Numbers tells the story of a generation who failed to trust their God. Caleb and Joshua had faithfully called the people to trust God and go take the Promised Land, but because of their fear, the majority voted against this action. God does not get out-voted. That generation had to die off to let the younger generation enter the land. More sin, more law, but in the midst of that, God restates His purpose, 'I am the LORD your God, who brought you out of the land of Egypt to be your God: I am the LORD your God.' (Num. 15:41)

As the next generation prepared to enter the land, Moses preached the book of Deuteronomy to them. It is a tremendous call to trust, to love, to remain devoted, to circumcise their hearts and live only for their God. As Moses came to the finale of his life and ministry, he presided over another renewal of the covenant, this time in Moab. In Deuteronomy 29, Moses reflected on the four decades of divine faithfulness and underlined the significance of that moment – God was making a covenant with them, 'that he may establish you today as his people, and that he may be your God, as he promised you, and as he swore to your fathers, to Abraham, to Isaac, and to Jacob.' (Deut. 29:13) He went on to speak to the people about the dangers of a drifting heart. Moses knew the people well and his warning was on target. In fact, God, who knew the people even better, confirmed Moses' fears that the people would break the covenant and whore after foreign gods (Deut. 31:16).

Things seemed to go well for a while. Joshua was a Moses-like leader with Moses-like success because of God's presence with him. But after the generally victorious campaign under Joshua, the story took a sad, but predictable, turn. The book of Judges is a catalogue of disaster: four centuries of unfaithfulness interspersed with divine deliverance through the most unlikely of deliverers. In Judges we see God using the fearful (Gideon threshing wheat in a winepress), the unlikely (a left-handed deliverer), the atypical (a woman stepping in where the man wimped out), the deeply troubled (super-strong Samson with his super-soft resolve), etc. These were not the best of times. And what was at the heart of the nation's problem in those days?

They did not listen to their judges, for they whored after other gods and bowed down to them (2:17). After Gideon made a golden ephod, we are told again, 'All Israel whored after it there' (8:27). After Gideon died, they let loose some more, 'the people of Israel turned again and whored after the Baals and made Baal-berith their god' (8:33). This was an era when the wife of the LORD was persistently promiscuous. As the start of the book of Chronicles surveys the history of the nation, the indictment is repeated, 'They broke faith with the God of their fathers, and whored after the gods of the peoples of the land, whom God had destroyed before them.' (1 Chron. 5:25)

When we move beyond the time of the Judges and into the times of the kings, we still find the same issues. If we fast-forward past the united monarchy into the time of the divided nation, we still find the language of marital unfaithfulness used of the people. For instance, King Jehoram led the nation of Judah into forsaking the LORD by building 'high places' where the people could play the whore with other gods. This brought an immediate reaction from Elijah who likened this whoring sin to that of the northern kingdom's evil whoring king Ahab (2 Chron. 21:10-13).

Once we get into the times of the kings, we have also arrived at the time of the prophets. Just like Elijah's letter to Jehoram, the other prophets all tend to put their finger on the real issue – unfaithfulness – as they address the state of the nation. In a later chapter we will spend time in the book of Hosea, the great book of outrageous grace overcoming whoring infidelity. The unfaithful people of God, called 'not my people' will again be 'my people' (see Hosea 1:9-10; 2:23).

One of the prophets, Isaiah, launches his great book with a courtroom scene in chapter 1. God is accusing His people of great sin and calling the heavens to listen to His case. What is His case? The people have proven deeply unfaithful to Him. They are like children that have rebelled against His loving care. They have despised Him and are estranged from Him. They are referred to as Sodom and Gomorrah, and their empty religious ritual is rejected. What was the heart of the issue? 'The faithful city has become a whore!' He even goes on to reference the oaks and the gardens of spiritual debauchery that they had desired and chosen over Him (Isa. 1, especially vv. 21 and 29). But by the end of the book, the city is dressed resplendently in robes of righteousness and is rejoiced over as a bride, a city not forsaken.

The next major prophet is even more overt. Jeremiah launches his great book with a stunning salvo of critiques fired against the unfaithful wife of the LORD. They were a people who had forsaken the LORD who had rescued them and 'on every high hill and under every green tree you bowed down like a whore.' (Jer. 2:19-20) They had worshipped at pagan shrines on every hill and in every grove of trees. The location of their idol worship might require explanation, but I suspect the vivid description of their actions does not. As God continues to speak through the prophet, He describes the people as a restless young camel and a wild donkey in heat with unrestrained lust – the language is shocking! (Jer. 2:23-24)

Jeremiah chapter 3 may be the ground zero passage for the biblical theme of spiritual adultery. God indicts the nation for playing the whore with many lovers. What man would take a wife back after she had done such as this? This wife of the LORD had been unfaithful on every hill that the eye could see; the whole land felt polluted now. Even with consequences raining down (or not, since rain showers had been withheld as discipline), still the brazen whore refused to be ashamed. (Jer. 3:1-3) Again, God spoke of Israel's faithlessness on every high hill and under every green tree, how she had played the whore. Judah, the sister of Israel, saw the brazen sin and its consequence, yet followed in the same footsteps. God's people were well and truly unfaithful to the God who had brought them into covenant with Him (Jer. 3:6-11).

Just as the prophets hold nothing back in their shocking description of the nation's sin, so the follow-up should knock us back in our seat. God the betrayed husband calls on His people to acknowledge their guilt and return to Him for mercy, for He would take them back. (Jer. 3:12-14) The prophets show us the hideous reality of human sin, but also the shocking grace flowing from God's good heart.

Jeremiah again speaks of the sin of God's people – faithlessness in response to God's goodness. 'When I fed them to the full, they committed adultery and trooped to the houses of whores. They were well-fed, lusty stallions, each neighing for his neighbor's wife.' (Jer. 5:7-8; see also 13:27 for the same imagery.) The effects of such sin were bearing down on the nation, and Jeremiah had the dubious privilege of declaring these forthcoming consequences. However, he also got to speak of God's great love and plans for His people beyond the discipline.

Jeremiah looked back to the establishment of the covenant, restating those glorious words, 'I will be your God, and you shall be my people …' (Jer. 7:23; 11:4); but the prophet's calling was to declare that the people had not been faithful. Jeremiah also had the privilege of looking beyond the forthcoming exile to see God's goodness in the future. He described God's plan to bring them back from exile and 'give them a heart to know that I am the LORD, and they shall be my people and I will be their God, for they shall return to me with their whole heart.' (Jer. 24:7, see also 30:22, as well as the great New Covenant passage, 31:33)

As we move into Ezekiel we find the same big theme pervades the book. The people are prone to abominable practices that demonstrate wayward hearts. They were whoring after other gods. (Ezek. 6:9) But God planned to bring the people back to the land, to give them a new heart and a new spirit. Bottom line? They will be faithful to God because of what He will do in them. They will be His people and He will be their God! (11:16-20; see also chapters 16, 23, 36 and 37, which we will look at in more detail in chapter 12 of this book.) Ezekiel is a thrilling book because the prophet is able to look beyond the present to the future resolution of the heart issues of God's people: the whoring will be dealt with, their hearts will be transformed and the new spirit God gives will bring the ultimate beautiful resolution. The whoring will be put away and God will dwell in the midst of His people! (See Ezek. 43:7-9; 48:35.)

The New Testament is the glorious culmination of many of these themes. How will God call wayward hearts into a close and intimate relationship? The New Testament makes explicit the plan that was gradually presented to the generations during the Old Testament. God's chosen and anointed servant, His deliverer redeemer would be His very own Son. So Jesus came and entered into the fullness of humanity that we might be drawn into the fullness of relationship with God. The New Testament is a glorious consummation of great Old Testament themes as we shall see in parts 3 and 4 of this book. First, in part 2, we shall take a more in depth look at the theme of marriage in the rest of the Old Testament.

God's central plan has always been to call out a bride for a marital covenant relationship with Christ. The New Testament offers that reality in rich multicolour. Now the dwelling place of God is even closer than before. Now 'we are the temple of the living God; as God said, "I will make my dwelling among them and walk among them, and I will be their God, and they shall be my people".' (2 Cor. 6:16)

As we finally reach the climax of the canon of Scripture, guess what we find? The biggest big idea is quoted again:

> 'And I saw the holy city, new Jerusalem, coming down out of heaven from God, prepared as a bride adorned for her husband. And I heard a loud voice from the throne saying, "Behold, the dwelling place of God is with man. He will dwell with them, and they will be his people, and God himself will be with them as their God".' (Rev. 21:2-3)

Part Two

A Faithful God, And …

Love is that powerful and prevalent passion, by which all the faculties and inclinations of the soul are determined, and on which both its perfection and happiness depend. The worth and excellency of a soul is to be measured by the object of its love.[1]

Henry Scougal

---

1. Henry Scougal, *The Life of God in the Soul of Man*, (Boston, Nichols & Notes: 1868), p. 40 (written originally in 1670s).

7 Black Velvet, Bright Diamond

• JUDGES AND RUTH

Wherefore, you being now married unto Christ, you must give all that you have of your own unto him; and truly you have nothing of your own but sin, and, therefore, you must give him that. I beseech you, then, say unto Christ with bold confidence, I give unto thee, my dear husband, my unbelief, my mistrust, my pride, my arrogancy, my ambition, my wrath, and anger, my envy, my covetousness, my evil thoughts, affections, and desires; I make one bundle of these and all my other offences, and give them unto thee.[1]

EDWARD FISHER

1. Edward Fisher, *The Marrow of Modern Divinity*, (Christian Focus, 2009, originally published in 1724), p. 167.

If I could do some rearranging in the Bible, I might be tempted to swap the blank page between Malachi and Matthew with the details given in the book of Judges. Both periods were roughly four centuries in length, both periods involved foreign oppression and divine deliverance, but would it be more edifying to have a book covering the period between the testaments instead of the depressing account of the times of the Judges?

Actually, as depressing as Judges is, it does play a powerful role in the biblical canon. Judges shows how quickly God's people can drift from Him. Judges also demonstrates how persistent God is in His pursuit of His people's affections. And Judges underlines the danger of neglecting our devotion to God.

There is one other benefit with Judges: it provides the black velvet backdrop for one of the brightest diamonds in the Bible – the book of Ruth.

Judges – The Dangerous Downward Spiral

Israel was in the land, but with Joshua and his generation gone, the horizon bore ominous clouds. Israel didn't drive out the pagan people as they had been warned to do. So now, God told them, these peoples would be thorns in their side, and their pagan gods would be a snare to them. Of course, God's predictions were accurate.

A generation arose who did not know the LORD, or the way He had delivered the nation. This was not simply a lack of cognitive knowledge; they lacked relational connection with Him. So the cycle begins in chapter 2 verse 11. Bear in mind that chapter 2 is an introductory overview of the pattern that would repeat many times throughout the book. Here is the cycle:

Sin (2:11-14) – They did evil in the sight of the LORD. Their crime was not cattle rustling or money laundering; they served the Baals – the false gods of the Canaanite people. What did this involve? The writer makes the sin clear in verses 12-14:

> And they abandoned the LORD, the God of their fathers, who had brought them out of the land of Egypt. They went after other gods, from among the gods of the peoples who were around them, and bowed down to them. And they provoked the LORD to anger. They abandoned the LORD and served the Baals and the Ashtaroth. So the anger of the LORD was kindled against Israel, …

The sin was spiritual adultery, and God's response was what you would expect from a deserted husband – anger.

Servitude (2:14-15) – Actually, God's response was not exactly what you might expect from a jilted husband. His anger did not result in the destruction of everyone involved, even though it initially would have appeared that way. God gave His people over to foreign attackers who came and plundered them. This does present a pretty bleak picture. In fact, God was against them; in every battle, He joined forces with the enemies of His people. But this was not revenge. It was part of His faithful plan to win their hearts back to Him …

Stress! (2:15c) – God was providentially working to bring His people to a point of real distress.

Save us! (2:18b) – So the deeply stressed people would groan and cry out to God because of their oppressors.

Saviour Sent (2:16 and 18a) – In answer to their groaning prayers for help, God would send a special saviour, a deliverer who would defeat the enemy and lead the people of God's nation. For a time, there was peace in the land.

Slipping (2:17) – But there was a problem with the people … ultimately, they would not listen to these God-sent deliverers. The reason is given very clearly: 'for they whored after other gods and bowed down to them.'

Sin (2:19) – So when each judge (or deliverer) died, the people would overtly turn as their hearts already implicitly had … 'after other gods, serving them and bowing down to them.'

This sin would, in turn, kindle God's anger and the cycle would repeat. *Sin. Servitude. Stress. Save us! Saviour Sent.* And *Slipping* again. In the final verses of the chapter God speaks of their unfaithfulness to His covenant. As a result, God determined to leave some nations in the land that Joshua had not driven out. The start of chapter 3 lists those nations, ending with an ominous comment:

> And their daughters they took to themselves for wives, and their own daughters they gave to their sons, and they served their gods. (3:6)

Intermarriage with pagans and spiritual adultery. Judges goes on to describe the worst of times, highlighting the miraculous and unusual deliverance God repeatedly provided through people like Othniel, Ehud and Shamgar, etc. Some of these accounts are very brief, but chapter 2 shows us the cycle that happened every time. This means that they didn't whore after false gods only once, but many times, even if the details aren't given in every situation.

The Cycle Spirals Down and Down

The depressing thing about Judges is that the people are so unresponsive to God. Just as soon as you read of the divinely appointed deliverer, you stumble immediately over the failure of the people. Their hearts were far from God and more loyal to the false gods of the Canaanite nations than to the God who was delivering them. Perhaps this is why we can relate to Judges, in spite of the bizarre stories it includes – because it describes the bizarre unfaithfulness of humans and our propensity to rebel against a loving God and chase after other lesser gods.

What is frightening about the book of Judges is how this pattern is repeated time and again. It is as if the people grew gradually harder and harder, more and more calloused to God, more and more hardened to His gracious pursuit of them. By the end of the book it is finally the shocking and disgusting event of a carved up concubine that stirs the nation into action (see chapters 19–20).

This parallels our lives. Loving sin as we do, we neglect God's goodness by drifting ever more ardently toward selfishness. Ultimately, we end up with seared consciences that require the most shocking event to stir a response in us – namely, the cut up body of Christ brutally displayed on the cross before our eyes. Whether we are new to the faith, or have walked with God for many years, we must beware of the adulterous drift of our affections. Sin hardens and desensitises our hearts. It takes the crucifixion to win hearts in the first place, and it takes regular return visits to the cross to protect us against a gradual hardening that can leave us cold toward God. The numbing effect of sin should frighten us. The crucifixion should shock us. The love of God is our only hope.

Heart-level Whoredom in Judges

One of the featured judges in the book was Gideon. His defeat of the Midianites with a vastly reduced army is popular in children's Bible storybooks (although they never tell the full story!) This wonderful God-orchestrated victory is concluded in chapter 8. Unsurprisingly, what follows the victory is profoundly, and worryingly, disappointing to read.

After his great victory, Gideon was invited to rule over the people of Israel. He refused, pointing the people toward God's rule. So far so good. Then he requested an amnesty on captured golden earrings, which he used to make a golden ephod. The ephod was a religious garment used by the priests to enquire of the LORD. Gideon seemed to like receiving guidance and perhaps wanted to have the guidance from God continue, but he was not honouring the established patterns of religious practice. He was not a Levite and thus not allowed to function as a priest. Ophrah was not the location of the tabernacle. And so the ephod became a snare – the whole nation 'whored after it there.' (See 8:27)

Instead of trusting in the LORD after their great victory, the nation immediately committed spiritual adultery by going after this religious object. Somehow their folk religion superstitiously panted for this special device, instead of the special God it was supposed to point toward (when kept in its proper context). So Gideon died, and immediately the people 'turned again and whored after the Baals and made Baal-berith their god'. (8:33) Baal-berith means 'Lord of the covenant' and seems to underline the fact that there was gross accommodation to the Canaanite gods going on. Maybe this particular Baal, at Shechem, seemed appropriate for the people of Israel … after all, their God was also 'Lord of the covenant.'

It is frightening to see how their whoring after other gods was not always in stark contrast to their worship of Yahweh. In this case they didn't worship a grotesque phallic symbol, but an item that actually should have been used in the context of true Yahweh worship. And the Baal they chose seemed to share some commonalities with their God. They were whoring after another god that looked a little bit like Yahweh. Perhaps He felt flattered. I suspect not.

There is a warning in this account for us. We probably don't struggle with the urge to make a golden ephod. But we are very capable of whoring after some element of Christianity, rather than remaining faithful to Christ Himself. Spiritual adultery is not only committed by pursuing a shockingly different religion, but also by forgetting our God and making some feature of church life or godly behaviour our focus. For example, when church attendance reassures us of our good spirituality, but we think very little of Christ Himself, perhaps we are whoring after an element of the Christian religion.

Ruth – The Bright Diamond

In the days when the judges judged we are introduced to Ruth and Boaz – a pair of glimmering godly diamonds set against the black velvet of the era of the judges. How could God's great plan to rescue His people traverse the four dismal centuries covered by the book of Judges? Surely any promised line would disappear in that mess. Actually, the book of Ruth finishes with that line that stretches forward from the book of Genesis to the arrival of the great King David.

Ruth starts with a woeful tale of death and despair. An Israelite, Elimelech (meaning My God is King), along with his wife, Naomi, and their two sons, left Bethlehem in a time of famine and headed to Moab. Bethlehem, which means the house of bread, was empty of provision for this couple, so they left the Promised Land and headed to enemy territory. There, tragedy continued to strike as Elimelech died, followed by the two sons. Naomi was left a widow with her two Moabite daughters-in-law.

Naomi heard that the LORD had been gracious to His people and provided food, so she set out to return to Bethlehem. One daughter-in-law returned to her family, but the other, Ruth, demonstrated great loyalty to Naomi and to the God of Naomi, and determined to come with her. The two women arrived in Bethlehem.

Naomi had two concerns at this point. The immediate concern was finding food to eat. The longer-term, and seemingly formidable issue was raising up an heir for her husband, which in those days would have been considered her greatest duty as a woman. In the second chapter the food issue was addressed. How? By God's quiet providence in leading Ruth to the field of good-guy Boaz. There are hints that marriage might occur too: there is no well (think back to Isaac, Jacob, etc.), but there is a character in a foreign land, a man asking the identity of a young lady, the drawing of water and a hospitable meal. Maybe something will happen here?

Naomi shifted focus from food to marriage and decided to play matchmaker. She wanted to try to force the hand of Boaz, a relative of her husband, with Ruth. Boaz could be their kinsman-redeemer – a relative able to buy back land and provide a male heir. God had worked out the food issue, now Naomi tried to play God in forcing the progeny issue.

Just as we tend to sanctify the stories in Judges for a younger audience in church Sunday Schools, so we tend to do the same with chapter 3 of Ruth, even for adults. Naomi's plan was obvious: get Ruth looking and smelling great, and then have her slip under the blanket late at night when Boaz was drunk. Things would happen and he would be obligated to take care of Ruth and any little ones that might possibly result from such a situation.

God had a better plan. In the dark days of the Judges, and the dark night of that harvest celebration, a godly man and a godly young lady remained pure in the most challenging of circumstances. Boaz, we discover later, was descended from Rahab and perhaps this played into his concern for Ruth's reputation (see Matt. 1:5).

So the final chapter plays out the story with Boaz redeeming Ruth, marrying her, and the baby coming legitimately. The story ends with Naomi holding this little one, who is then referred to as her kinsman-redeemer (4:14-15), pointing forward to his descendant, David.

The story of Ruth and Boaz shines all the more brightly because of the context in which it occurred. It is as if God wants His unfaithful wife, Israel, to taste the beauty of godly marriage along the way. God is a truly wonderful husband, but will His wife ever reciprocate with godly faithfulness? It took a Moabitess – a non-Israelite – to make the story work, so perhaps that says something about the sorry state of God's chosen nation. Would things improve in the coming time of kings and prophets?

8 Royal Weddings and Scandals

DAVID AND SOLOMON

To have the love of one who is altogether lovely, to know that the glorious Majesty of heaven hath any regard unto us, how it must astonish and delight us! How must it overcome our spirits and melt our hearts, and put our whole soul into a flame! [1]

HENRY SCOUGAL

My God, spiritualise my affections! Give me to know what it is to have the intense and passionate love of Christ. Let me find of this love that it is better than all earthly desires and gratifications. Draw me, O God, to Christ. [2]

THOMAS CHALMERS

---

1. Henry Scougal, *The Life of God in the Soul of Man,* p. 109.
2. Thomas Chalmers, *Posthumous Works of Thomas Chalmers*, Vol. 3 (T. Constable, 1852), p. 251.

If the times of the Judges were the worst of times, then the times of David and Solomon were seen as the best of times. The final judge and prophet, Samuel, oversaw the transition to having a monarchy in Israel. First, the people's choice was tall King Saul, who was rejected by God. Then came God's choice, young David – a man after God's own heart.

The books of Samuel tell the story from Samuel to Saul to David. The anointed David had to survive the attacks of Saul for many years, but eventually he ruled in Hebron and then Jerusalem (1 Sam. 16-31 and 2 Sam. 1-5). He brought the Ark of the Covenant back to Jerusalem, received the great promise of God to establish his descendant on his throne forever (2 Sam. 6-7), and continued to be victorious over the surrounding nations in battle (2 Sam. 8-10).

God's promise to David was a glorious covenant on a par with the one He made earlier with Abraham and that He made later in the New Covenant. In the aftermath of God's great promise to him, David blew it. He was a great king, but in his middle years he failed to be a good man. David didn't meet his wives by a well, but each time there was a story marred by violence. Michal and Abigail may not always get a mention, but David's life story is never told without reference to the time he looked from the balcony of his palace and saw the beautiful Bathsheba (2 Sam. 11-12). He saw. He desired. He took. He lied. He killed. And for the next chapters we read the sad story of the unraveling of David's family as the consequences played out.

King David knew personally the power of male-female attraction, the beauty of marriage, the ugliness of adultery, and the consequences of sin. And in his Psalms, he traced these themes upward from humans to God Himself.

Psalms: The Songbook of the Messiah

The book of Psalms is a richly crafted collection of poems pointing ultimately to the greater son of David, the Messiah who would eventually come and reign. For instance, the collection begins with two Psalms that set the tone for all that follows. On a human level, the first Psalm demonstrates that there are two types of people – those who listen to the world, and the individual who meditates on God's Word; their destinies are very different. On a grander scale, the destiny of the nations of the world is described in the second Psalm. The nations may rage against the throne of God and His Anointed ruler, but God just laughs at their petulance. He establishes His Son, the King, on His throne and that settles things forever. So the kings of the nations are warned:

10 Now therefore, O kings, be wise;
   be warned, O rulers of the earth.

11 Serve the LORD with fear,
   and rejoice with trembling.

12 Kiss the Son,
   lest he be angry, and you perish in the way,
   for his wrath is quickly kindled.
      Blessed are all who take refuge in him.

This Psalm highlights the central question in our lives – how will we interact with the Son? But what does it mean to kiss Him? Is this a kiss of affection, or a kissing of the ring of a king to signify subservient devotion? However we might take Psalm 2, when we come to another royal Psalm, number 45, the marital theme becomes evident.

The Wedding Song

At first glance the Psalm is a wedding song celebrating the marriage of an Israelite king and his bride. But there is a curious reference to God in verse 6. Thus the Psalm came to be seen by many as referring to a wedding of God Himself with Israel as His bride. Since the Psalms often point forward to the coming Messiah, maybe all these ideas come together – this is the Son of God, the Messiah, being united to His bride in holy matrimony.

The Psalm praises the groom through to verse 9, and then switches to praise the bride until verse 15, with a couple of concluding verses expressing hope that the king's dynasty would continue into the future to finish the Psalm.

The groom is celebrated as the best of men, anointed with grace by God Himself (see 45:2,7). He is a champion for the cause of truth, humility and righteousness, a majestic victor over his enemies, celebrated by the daughters of kings. This king adorns his royal bride with the finest gold.

Therefore the bride is also praised from verse 10. She leaves her own people to be desired by the king. She bows to him. Because of who she now is, she is celebrated as the glorious bride with her attendants.

So who is this groom, and therefore, who is this bride? The language seems too elevated for it to be simply referring to a king of Israel and his bride (although they did elevate language in reference to the king). But lest we assume the reference to God in verse 6 is mere hyperbole, don't miss the last line: 'therefore nations will praise you forever and ever.' In the Psalms, the image of the 'peoples' or 'nations' praising someone is always referring to the praise of Yahweh, never a mere human.

Perhaps the original setting of the Psalm focused on a human royal wedding, but in time the people of Israel saw the Psalm as more than a nostalgic throwback to the good old days of royal weddings in the land. Certainly by the time they were in exile, this Psalm was seen to anticipate the coming Messiah and His bride. By the time of the New Testament, this Psalm was being applied to Christ. In Hebrews 1:8-9, the writer states that it is speaking of the Son. When we get to Revelation 19, we see John using the language of the Psalm as Christ rides forth valiantly and majestically to put down His enemies (Rev. 19:11-16), which is why the bride is urged to clothe herself with white linens (Rev. 19:6-8).

This means that we can enter into the greater wedding depicted in this Psalm and praise the glorious majesty and splendid victories of God's king, our groom. We can, even now, be dressing ourselves in the white linens, which are the righteous acts of the saints.

Solomon – The Marriage Writer

If we are going to look at the theme of marriage between God and humanity through the Scriptures, then many would consider the Song of Solomon to be the place to go. This love poem has, for centuries, been viewed as a picture of God and His bride, of Christ and the church.

Part of the reason for this interpretation is that the poetry goes beyond the romantic to the explicit and erotic, which has left medieval monks and modern evangelicals alike feeling slightly awkward. In fact, our English translations still soften elements that would surprise us if they were translated more overtly.

A. The Song begins with the courtship (1:1–3:5). The young lady is longing for love, but the story began with her riddled with insecurity. He, the lover-king, declared that she is superlatively beautiful, speaking words of affirmation and desire that drew her into reciprocating with praise for him. She is amazed by his love, 'he brought me to the banqueting house, and his banner over me was love!' she declares (2:4). The power of his embrace stirs something deep within her, and she warns the daughters of Jerusalem not to awaken love until the right time (this becomes the refrain of the book: 2:7; 3:5; 8:4). The poem continues to describe a playful visit to the country as her security grows in his love – 'My beloved is mine, and I am his' (2:16). Yet at night the insecurities remain, and the refrain is repeated.

B. The Song then describes the wedding (3:6–5:1). Now we discover the groom is King Solomon, arriving in all of his splendour. Chapter 4 traces the wedding night and the consummation of the marriage – again he initiates by describing her naked beauty, she is 'altogether beautiful' and without flaw. So he celebrates her captivating love, and the beauty of her purity. Finally, their marriage is consummated.

C. Following the wedding comes a description of the marriage maturing (5:2–8:4). There seem to be problems, for he is absent. But as she returns to praising him, so she returns to the wonder of their intimacy and they are reconciled (see chapters 5–6). So the husband praises his wife again, celebrating her beauty and the privilege of shared intimacy. And in return she rejoices, 'I am my beloved's and his desire is for me.' (7:10) As they interact with each other lovingly, so their desire for greater intimacy grows.

D. The Song comes to a conclusion with a declaration about the great power of love – it is as strong as death and many waters cannot quench it (8:5-7). Finally there is an epilogue looking back to how the great love began between Solomon and his bride. (8:8-14).

So is this song about God and His people, even Christ and the church? Or is it telling a historical story of a country girl wooed and won by the stranger who captivates her, and marries her? If we insist that it is only describing 'divine marriage' then we may not be fully honouring the original intent of the biblical author. Perhaps this reveals an assumption that God could not have wanted such an explicit celebration of human marriage. (When people interpret the text allegorically, often they will assign meanings to the text and dismiss the plain meaning of the text – this can make it look like God is not a trustworthy or clear communicator.)

If we insist that it is only describing a human story of love and marriage, then we may be ignoring the greater image that all marriage points to – that of God's plan to draw out a bride for His Son.

Perhaps the best approach is to first recognise the human story and appreciate that God delights in marital sexuality (notice that the lovers genuinely enjoy each other – this is not some sort of 'procreation only' stoic view of marital intimacy). Then second, because all marriage points to the marriage between God's Son and God's people, appreciate the richness of this divine marriage understanding of the Song.

Indeed, Christ does pursue His bride, delight in her, and bring her to His banqueting table, covering her with His love. What a privilege to be wooed and won by the Son of God Himself!

Solomon's Other Marital Writing

Solomon didn't just pen the wonderful Song of all songs. He also led the charge on the archetypal wisdom book, Proverbs. We tend to think of Proverbs as a collection of two-line sayings that offer pithy observational insight into matters of money, character, wisdom, relationships, and so on.

But don't miss the way the book is framed. For the first nine chapters, a father trains his son for the challenges of life. The father urges his son to fear the LORD, which is the beginning of wisdom, and sets before him an image of two women – Lady Wisdom and Lady Folly.

Will he pursue Lady Wisdom? She cries aloud in the streets (1:20-21) and invites the foolish young to listen to her. Those who don't will reap disastrous fruit. But the father urges his son to respond to Lady Wisdom – for wisdom is given by the LORD. (2:1-15)

Or will he be trapped by Lady Folly, the Harlot? This adulterous covenant breaker lures young and foolish men to certain destruction (2:16-19).

Because of the personification of wisdom in these chapters, some have seen an implicit reference to Christ Himself – the One who comes forth from the Father, the One who created all things. (See 3:19-20.) So the early chapters of Proverbs continue to extol the virtues of wisdom and the dangers of the adulteress. This wise father tells his son that the greatest need of all is his need to guard his heart, because from it flow all the issues of life (see 4:23).

The father describes the seductive lure of the adulteress, along with the certain destruction that she brings (5:1-14; see also 6:20-35; 7:1-27 even describes seduction by a harlot). The father encourages his son to be faithful to the wife of his youth, describing the delight of sexual and emotional intimacy with her as opposed to the harlot (5:15-23). The wonder of wisdom is offered again in the personified speech of chapter 8 – so lofty that many see Christ in these words, even if the text does not require this understanding. Chapter 9 again sets forth the two ladies in summary – wisdom and folly. Which one will the reader choose?

Interestingly, the book ends with another extended poem in chapter 31, this time to the wife of noble character and her value. While some will read this and see a pattern for godly femininity with all its strengths and characteristics, others will struggle with the apparently exaggerated nature of the description, finding it to be an impossible standard to live up to rather than a beautiful inspirational picture. Perhaps we should read this poem as a framing of the book, reminding us of the blessing of pursuing marriage to Lady Wisdom, instead of the death-dealing destructive faithlessness offered by the harlot. If the poem can inspire godly femity, that is great, but if the description seems overwhelming then remember that we are to look to Christ to grow us, not to ourselves and our own efforts to mature.

The Irony of Solomon

Ironically, Solomon brings us the Song and the two women of Proverbs, but his own life experience of marriage brought him to ruin. Solomon's reign really was the golden age of Israel. David had finished the wars leaving peace and prosperity for his son, Solomon. God appeared to Solomon and blessed him with incredible wealth and riches after Solomon asked only for the wisdom to rule well. This wisest of human kings had everything he could have wanted. He built the magnificent temple for God and prayed a wonderfully rich prayer of dedication (see 1 Kings 8). For ten whole chapters,

Solomon is ticking every box as a great and wonderful king for God's people. Then comes 1 Kings chapter 11.

Even with all the advantages that he had, Solomon ultimately failed. Why? Marriage. Lots of marriages. First Kings 11 explains how Solomon didn't guard his own heart. Instead he loved many foreign women, and with them, their gods. He was a spiritual adulterer. The wisest man ever still fell for the wrong woman. Oh the power of the human heart! Why do we think we can outwit our hearts with our heads? Even Solomon couldn't do that.

So ultimately Solomon's glorious reign ended in ignominy, and the nation subsequently divided into two. The emotions wrapped up in marriage are so powerful. Beautiful when kept ordered according to God's ordering of relationship, but volatile and dangerous when we play with unrestricted fire. Maybe it has to be this way.

Perhaps the power of attraction and of marriage, as well as the extreme joy and pain that can be caused in this sphere of life, is exactly what it needs to be. That is, the beauty and wonder of what God wants for us will be so glorious that we have to experience the power of it now, even though this fallen world will corrupt so much of the goodness. Marriage can thrill, and if corrupted it can devastate, because it is the ultimate taster of what we were made for. Response to His pursuit will ultimately lead to the most satisfyingly intimate and loving relationship with the life-giving God. Rejection of God in favour of other lovers will only bring the most agonising emptiness and destruction.

9   Marry Who?

• HOSEA

Rather than a violation of God's moral order, what we observe here is 'one of the most remarkable depictions of divine grace in the Old Testament.' [1]

RAY ORTLUND, JR.

O to grace how great a debtor daily I'm constrained to be!
Let Thy goodness, like a fetter, bind my wandering heart
   to Thee.
Prone to wander, Lord, I feel it, prone to leave the God
   I love;

---

1. Ray Ortlund Jr., *God's Unfaithful Wife: A Biblical Theology of Spiritual Adultery* (Downers Grove, IL: IVP Apollos, 1996), p. 50, citing T. E. McComiskey.

Here's my heart, O take and seal it, seal it for Thy courts
above.[2]

ROBERT ROBINSON,
Come, Thou Fount of Every Blessing

Hosea is heartbreaking. This is because Israel herself was heartbreaking. Hosea was called to not only speak for God, but also to live out his message for God in a dramatic way. Hosea was called to marry a wife given to whoredom. This was because God had done the same thing.

The book is easy to survey, but devastating to study. Chapters 1–3 tell Hosea and Gomer's story. Then in 4:1 Hosea complains that in Israel there is no faithfulness, no steadfast love and no knowledge of God. These themes are then pursued in reverse order. There is no knowledge of God (chapters 4–5); no steadfast love (chapters 6–11); and no faithfulness (chapters 12–14). As the book progresses, each section ends with the brighter dawning of hope for the future in the mercy of God (6:1-3; 11:1-11; 14:1-9). That's the survey, but now let's enter into the story.

Hosea lived in the northern kingdom of Israel in the eighth century before Christ. He was a contemporary of Isaiah who lived in the southern kingdom of Judah. Hosea lived in the final years of the northern kingdom, leading up to their defeat at the hands of Assyrian ruler, Sargon II in 721 B.C. The northern kingdom had experienced a succession of dynasties and kings, every one of them doing evil in the eyes of the LORD. The southern kingdom had eight good kings over the years and thus lasted a century longer before divine discipline would also remove them from the land.

---

2. Robert Robinson, *Come, Thou Fount of Every Blessing*, 1758.

Hosea lived among an unfaithful people. The land was divided between rich and poor. The law courts were corrupt and there had been a major breakdown in public morality. Their religion was horribly blended with Baal worship – the Canaanite storm and fertility gods that Israel seemed to readily mix in with superficial worship of their own 'master', Yahweh. The nation was committing spiritual adultery. Hosea was called to experience in his own life and marriage what God felt in His.

Hosea presents a profoundly relational portrait of God. He is a father lovingly caring for His son as he takes his first steps (11:1-12). He is a physician ready to heal the nation (6:1; 7:1; 11:3; 14:4). He is a shepherd providing for His flock (13:5-6). But most of all, God is a jilted husband, faithfully pursuing His unfaithful and whoring wife, wooing her (2:14-15), marrying her (2:2, 16), providing for her (2:8), cherishing and loving her with all His heart (11:8), and knowing her in the wilderness (13:5).

Israel had a token religiosity, but she didn't really know God. He certainly wasn't seen to be sufficient for her and so her 'spirit of whoredom' led her away from the God to whom she was married by covenant.

> My people inquire of a piece of wood,
> and their walking staff gives them oracles.
> For a spirit of whoredom has led them astray,
> and they have left their God to play the whore.
>
> They sacrifice on the tops of the mountains
> and burn offerings on the hills,
> under oak, poplar, and terebinth,
> because their shade is good.
> Therefore your daughters play the whore,
> and your brides commit adultery. (4:12-13)

Let's slow down through the first three chapters, the story of Hosea and Gomer.

The Prophet's Family (1:2-2:1)

The sordid tale begins with God's instruction to Hosea, that he should take a wife of whoredom and have children of whoredom, because the land of Israel was committing whoredom by forsaking the LORD. Whoredom is an old word that is stronger than adultery, and sadly it is the right word to use of the faithlessness described in this book. Apparently without hesitation, Hosea obeyed God's instruction. Some think that Gomer was at this point already a prostitute plucked from the life by Hosea. Others view her as a wife with a propensity toward unfaithfulness. Either way, Hosea knew what he was getting into. He knew her heart would stray, and with it, her body. He knew to anticipate heartache. And thus, he knew how God felt about His people.

How God felt about His people grew clearer as He instructed Hosea to name a sequence of children with symbolic meanings. The first little one was Jezreel, a place notorious for bloodshed. Israel was soon to be destroyed in battle.

The next little one was a daughter, No-Mercy. God had seen enough of Israel to determine that the time had come for Him to stop showing mercy. To make matters worse, Judah, across the border, would receive mercy from Yahweh, their God. Some of His people there were still faithful. In fact, Judah would receive deliverance from the great Assyrian threat based purely on God's mercy – not their army strength, nor their political alliances, just God's mercy.

Lastly, Gomer bore another son. He was pithily named Not-My-People. So this was it? A 'Dear John' note from God? Israel had been so overwhelmingly unfaithful to the covenant that the relationship was ended. I am not my beloved's. He is not mine. It is over. Finished. Can there be any pain as deep as the breakdown of a marriage?

Hosea immediately offers hope, establishing a pattern that will continue throughout the book. Devastating failure, then the dawn of future hope. Human sin, divine grace. He points back to the language of the covenant, and forward to the hope of an innumerable people. The Not-My-People shall be called 'Children of the living God.' Jezreel's day will be great, and to the brothers it will be said, 'You are my people!' And to the sisters it will be said, 'You have received mercy!'

Hosea is an emotional rollercoaster, and it has only just begun.

The Pain of Faithlessness (2:2-13)

God is ready to spell out the whoredom of Israel in 2:2-13. Israel's whoring makes a joke of Yahweh, and understandably, He is angry.

He disowns her and threatens judgment, yet all the while offering her the opportunity to turn back to Him. In fact, things are so bad, that the appeal has to be communicated through the children (the individuals), to their mother (the nation). He wants her to remove the adultery from between her breasts – to take away the Baals from between her towns. She may have dressed seductively, but He is ready to strip her completely naked and turn her into a desert. (2:2-3)

A typical prostitute would let the men approach her, but Israel determined to pursue her clientele. Israel believed that these lovers could provide what she needed. The tangibility of the Baals seemed to serve the selfish needs of Israel; they thought these idols could provide fertility in the field and in the home. (2:4-5)

7 She shall pursue her lovers
    but not overtake them,
and she shall seek them
    but shall not find them.
Then she shall say,
    'I will go and return to my first husband,
    for it was better for me then than now.'

8 And she did not know
    that it was I who gave her
    the grain, the wine, and the oil,
and who lavished on her silver and gold,
    which they used for Baal.

9 Therefore I will take back
    my grain in its time,
    and my wine in its season,
and I will take away my wool and my flax,
    which were to cover her nakedness. (2:7-9)

In these verses God thwarts the apparent benefits of Baal worship, but Israel continues to pursue these other lovers for a while. They absolutely fail her. Actually, it is the LORD who makes sure Israel's whoredom can never succeed. Out of selfish appetite, Israel will determine to return to her first husband. He, after all, did provide for her, even if she did not realise it. God and God alone was sufficient to care for Israel, even though Israel bizarrely used what He gave for the worship of Baal. How can we take what is given by God and give it away to other lovers in acts of spiritual adultery? Maybe we act in this same way at times.

God is ready to deal with the sin of unfaithfulness. The partying is over, the wages of harlotry are finished. The promised curses of Deuteronomy 28 are being readied for action as reality is about to hit home for the faithless wife of Yahweh. She put all her effort into dressing up to attract these inert other lovers, but she forgot the all-sufficient LORD. (2:10-13)

The Wonder of Divine Grace! (2:14-23)

'Therefore, behold, I will allure her, and bring her
    into the wilderness,
and speak tenderly to her.' (2:14)

The anger of God is totally understandable. But the grace of God is astonishing! He plans to lead her from prosperity to the wilderness – not to punish, but to woo her again. Israel was closer to the LORD when she had just been delivered from Egypt, so God's plan was to put her in that vulnerable place once again.

16 'And in that day, declares the LORD, you will call me "My Husband," and no longer will you call me "My Baal." 17 For I will remove the names of the Baals from her mouth, and they shall be remembered by name no more. 18 And I will make for them a covenant on that day with the beasts of the field, the birds of the heavens, and the creeping things of the ground. And I will abolish the bow, the sword, and war from the land, and I will make you lie down in safety. 19 And I will betroth you to me forever. I will betroth you to me in righteousness and in justice, in steadfast love and in mercy. 20 I will betroth you to me in faithfulness. And you shall know the LORD.' (2:16-20)

And so the Baals will be forgotten. Yahweh will no longer be half-followed and called by the name of Israel's other lover –

'master.' Israel will be betrothed in righteousness, in love, in mercy, in faithfulness. Israel will know the LORD. This is more than head knowledge. This is intimate and loyal communion. The section concludes with another reference to the children's names. God will have mercy on No-Mercy, and Not-My-People will be 'My-People' and they will call Him 'My God.' Hosea is looking forward to a new marriage that will be entirely more successful. There is overlap here in theme and wording with the New Covenant promises of Jeremiah and Ezekiel … God will establish an entirely better forever relationship!

Hosea's Godly Calling (3:1-5)

Hosea, like God, would be tempted to merely tolerate a wayward wife. Tolerate. Accept. Receive. Language that could be used of God's relationship with us, if it weren't for the biblical insistence that God actually loves us. So Hosea was called to proactively pursue, woo, and win his wife back. That is a godly calling.

His wife was long gone. She no longer came home to him after her liaisons. Gomer was now past her prime and was giving herself to her current lover. Hosea had to go to the market, spot his wife, and pay a price for her. She wasn't worth much now. He paid fifteen shekels and some barley.

Hosea brought Gomer home. She had to be told to stay faithful. He graciously promised that he would be too.

So the story part of Hosea concludes with the prophet pointing forward to Israel's future return to seek the LORD their God. Like Hosea, God would eventually win Israel back to Himself.

Where is the Knowledge of God? (Chapters 4-5)

In the Old Testament, to know someone is a profoundly marital concept. We may live in a knowledge-as-data culture, but that is not the biblical notion. Adam knew Eve and she conceived. To know someone is profoundly relational, even marital.

Through the prophet, in chapter 4, God goes after both the people and the priests. The latter especially should have been sources of knowledge about God so that the nation could have relational knowledge of God. Instead, the priests led the nation into forgetting the law and forsaking God. Godlessness was rampant. The nation was whoring, both literally and spiritually. So God predicts punishment in chapter 5. Eventually the nation will turn back to the healing goodness of God. They will recognise that their greatest need is to know Him.

Where is the Steadfast Love? (Chapters 6-11)

Probably the most powerful single word in the Old Testament is '*hesed*' – lovingkindness, steadfast or loyal love. Israel needed to be gripped by steadfast love, but instead their love was mere mist. God wanted steadfast love rather than empty religious ritual (6:6). Indeed, the godlessness of the nation was, by definition, the very opposite of godly covenant loyalty. Everyone was out for themselves. Israel sought the help of other nations, all because she had forgotten her Maker. In fact, God had pursued Israel, but they had given themselves over to the Baal Peor. As a result, they became detestable, like the thing they loved (see 9:10). Love is always the issue, and its direction is always critical.

So after chapters of depressing description of their faithlessness, we come to chapter 11. The people of Israel can't manufacture steadfast love, but the LORD can remind them of it. God loved Israel in the past; He led them with cords of kindness and with bands of love (11:4).

Where is the Faithfulness? (Chapters 12-14)

Many times in the Old Testament, we find steadfast love (*hesed*) paired with faithfulness (*emet*). This pairing comes out as 'grace and truth' in the New Testament, but the Old Testament context underlines the loyal nature of this term (as opposed to the factual nature of our word 'truth'). Essentially God promises to be forever loving, and forever true. He keeps that promise.

Israel was anything but faithful. Israel was like a morning mist, or morning dew, or chaff swirling in the threshing floor, or smoke from a window (13:3). There, then gone. But God is the exact opposite. He always was, always is, and always will be true and trustworthy. Chapter 14 offers the final glorious glimpse of God's goodness to come.

> I will heal their apostasy;
> > I will love them freely,
> > for my anger has turned from them. (14:4)

And vv. 7-8:

> They shall return and dwell beneath my shadow;
> > they shall flourish like the grain;
> they shall blossom like the vine;
> > their fame shall be like the wine of Lebanon.
> O Ephraim, what have I to do with idols?
> > It is I who answer and look after you.
> I am like an evergreen cypress;
> > from me comes your fruit. (14:7-8)

Centuries later, Peter wrote his first epistle to Christians who had been exiled from Rome to Turkey. Their circumstances were so discouraging, but the truth of the gospel offered wonderful comfort. Peter wrote, 'You are a chosen race, a royal priesthood, a holy nation, a people for his own possession … Once you were not a people, but now you are God's people; once you had not received mercy, but now you have received mercy.' (1 Pet. 2:9-10). Hosea's message lasted long beyond his own time!

God is faithful, and God is sufficient. Hosea portrays the wonder of God as our husband in ways that bring tears, bring praise, and bring hope. In fact, the other prophets also pick up the great theme of marriage, the wonder of having God as husband. Let's chase this theme through a few of the prophetic books.

10 **My Delight Is In Her**

• ISAIAH

In a married condition there is a mutual, entire love. That is, loving the person more than the benefits received from him. True conjugal love is fixed on the persons, rather than on the estates, or any thing they enjoy by them. So, on Christ's part, his love is fixed on the persons of the saints, more than on their actions. It is true, all the gracious actions you do are lovely before Christ, for they are the fruits of his Spirit; but Christ's greatest love is toward your persons. So your chiefest love, if it be a true conjugal affection, settles on the person of Christ rather than on any thing derived from him. Notwithstanding those riches of pardon of sin and precious promises which thou enjoyest through him, his person is that which ravishes thy soul.[1]

JEREMIAH BURROUGHS

As Hosea was tasting the depth of God's grace in the northern kingdom, Isaiah was eloquently preaching it in the southern kingdom. Like Hosea, Isaiah had a message from God for a people who were unfaithful to Him and proactive in their pursuit of foreign alliances and sinful living. Like Hosea, Isaiah had a message of hope beyond God's present condemnation of the people's spiritual infidelity. And like Hosea, Isaiah had special insight into the great idea of God being the husband of His people.

Isaiah's ministry spanned many decades. He began as Assyria were breathing down the neck of every king in the region, soon defeating Israel and eventually coming to the very doorstep of Jerusalem. But then Isaiah also saw the first predictions of the coming threat from Babylon. His ministry offered contemporary insight, as well as anticipation of the coming exile, the coming Messiah, the coming day of the Lord, and the future new heavens and new earth.

The faithful city has become a …

The great book of Isaiah is launched with a courtroom scene. The people of God stand accused of great sin. God is the accuser. The heavens and the earth are the jury. And what is the accusation? Whereas animals know their owners, Israel does not know nor understand her God. The nation has forsaken God and is utterly estranged from Him. They might be continuing their religious rituals, but the LORD is

---

1. Jeremiah Burroughs, *An Exposition of Hosea* (Edinburgh: James Nichols, 1863), p. 160.

sick of all that since it has no meaning. Bottom line? 'The faithful city has become a whore!' (1:21)

God is going to do something that involves both judgment and restoration. The result will be that Jerusalem will be called 'the city of righteousness, the faithful city'. (1:26) For those who do not repent, there will be judgment. For those that do repent and turn back to God, there will come a time when they will look back ashamed and embarrassed that they cavorted with false fertility gods in the groves of trees.

The first five chapters of Isaiah offer a background to the state of the nation in his day. He starts with the courtroom scene, and ends with a moving song of the vineyard, transitioning into a set of woes against the wicked (chapter 5). The love song of the vineyard uses language reminiscent of Song of Solomon until it becomes clear that this vineyard is in rebellion against the one who has cared for her.

Sweeping through Isaiah

After the five-chapter background, Isaiah is called to his ministry in chapter 6 – a ministry that will be tough and unfruitful. Thankfully, despite the unresponsiveness of the nation, Isaiah's book is rich with hope-filled content for us to enjoy. He presents the Immanuel section – anticipating the coming of the child who is God with us (chapters 7–12), he presents burdens against the surrounding nations (chapters 13–23) and then comes to his mini-apocalypse – anticipating the future feasting of God's people and God's swallowing of death itself (chapters 24–27). Isaiah offers a more contemporary proof of his message by focusing on the current events of his day concerning the northern nation of Israel and Egypt (chapters 28–35). Then in the middle section of the book, he describes the end of the Assyrian threat and predicts the Babylonian exile (chapters 36–37 and 38–39 respectively).

When we come to chapter 40, we really step on to the most hallowed of Old Testament ground. We read of the LORD's vast superiority to the deaf, blind, dumb and inert gods of Babylon – the Creator is the Lord of history (chapters 40–48). We read of the Servant of the LORD and His self-sacrificial mission to pay the penalty for sin – the Redeemer is Saviour of all (chapters 49–57). We read of the Spirit-filled Messiah and the dawning of a new age of hope for God's people and all of creation – the Sovereign Ruler will establish righteousness in the last days (chapters 58–66).

Your Mother Was A ...

In chapter 57, Isaiah offers another bleak insight into the unfaithfulness of the nation. Even though the righteous people are being persecuted, these godly ones are able to rest in their beds (v. 1-2). However, the idolaters rush headlong into every kind of spiritual unfaithfulness (vv. 3-13). These people are in trouble by their lineage – their mother is called both a witch and an adulterous harlot (57:3); but they are also guilty by their own participation ... lusting under every green tree for the false gods typically presented there (57:5). While the righteous man can sleep at night, the idolater fornicates on his bed with other lovers (57:7-8). Ultimately, these idols could do nothing for these people, but God would! (57:13)

The Nature of the Covenant

Isaiah is rich with hope for God's people. For instance, the four songs of the servant of Yahweh point to the identity and mission of this individual who will establish justice on earth

(42:1-4): He will bring salvation to the ends of the earth (49:1-6); He will faithfully sustain the weary (50:4-9); and He will carry our griefs and die for our sins (52:13–53:12). These are real highlight sections of Isaiah, but don't miss what follows these songs.

The Servant is the covenant – After the first two servant songs, Isaiah refers to the caring concern of God and the way He gives the Servant as a covenant for the people (see 42:6; 49:8). Where Jeremiah and Ezekiel will lay out the details of the New Covenant that God will make in the future, Isaiah makes it clear that the New Covenant plan is wrapped up in an individual, the Servant who will come and die.

The Invitation to trust the LORD – After the third servant song, there is an invitation to trust in the LORD, to rely on Him alone, rather than any of the false gods that others were sacrificing to in that time (50:10-11).

The eternal covenant is marital – After the fourth servant song, there is an extended celebration of the covenant that God is making with His people. They need not fear, for shame will be taken away, and the reproach of their widowhood will be forgotten.

> For your Maker is your husband,
> the LORD of hosts is his name;
> and the Holy One of Israel is your Redeemer,
> the God of the whole earth he is called. (54:5)

The passage goes on to describe the brief separation and ultimate restoration that we saw in Hosea.

'For the LORD has called you
    like a wife deserted and grieved in spirit,
like a wife of youth when she is cast off,
    says your God.
For a brief moment I deserted you,
    but with great compassion I will gather you.
In overflowing anger for a moment
    I hid my face from you,
but with everlasting love I will have compassion on you,'
    says the LORD, your Redeemer. (54:6-8)

God commits to no longer being angry with His people. Instead,

'This is like the days of Noah to me:
    as I swore that the waters of Noah
    should no more go over the earth,
so I have sworn that I will not be angry with you,
    and will not rebuke you.
For the mountains may depart
    and the hills be removed,
but my steadfast love shall not depart from you,
    and my covenant of peace shall not be removed,'
    says the LORD, who has compassion on you. (54:9-10)

So God's steadfast love, His covenant-loyal-love will be forever set on the bride. This is no contractual arrangement between God and humanity. As we have mentioned previously, some like to see two-sided contractual covenants throughout the Bible, but this is one of many places where covenant language is used in the context of the forever love commitment of marriage. This is not about stipulation, obedience and reward.

This is about a God putting Himself into covenant marriage with His people – now that gives us profound security!

The Songs of the Conqueror

In the final section of Isaiah we find another four poems, this time dedicated to the Conqueror, but running parallel to the earlier Servant Songs. Like in the first servant song, this Conqueror appears suddenly, and He is anointed by God's Spirit to speak the Words of God (59:20-21). Like in the second Servant Song, He has a double task: this time to bring good news and vengeance (61:1-3). Like in the third Servant Song, the Anointed Conqueror tells of His commitment to doing the will of the LORD (61:10–62:7). And like in the fourth Servant Song, the arm of the LORD is revealed, only now in the conquering and vengeance of the Anointed Conqueror (63:1-6).

These four poems are also followed by rich comment, this time underlining the identity of God's people as a result of what His Anointed will have achieved. First, Jerusalem will be God's city, the centre of pilgrimage for all nations (see Isaiah 60). Second, God's people will be God's priests, receiving the wealth of nations and bound to the LORD by covenant (61:4-9). Third, they will be married to God, delighted in and rejoiced over by God Himself (62:2-12). Fourth, they will be God's people, His children, recipients of God's steadfast love (63:7-19).

It is that third poem, and its following comments, that we must dwell on before we finish this chapter. In 61:10, Isaiah describes the special clothing given to the nation by God – the robe of righteousness. He also mentions the bridegroom dressing up for the occasion, along with the bride. The wedding dress in this passage is the radiant righteousness that is given to the city. God's people will no longer be known as Forsaken, or Desolate. Instead they will be called Hephzibah, which means My Delight is in Her, and the land will go by the name of Married. Just to be clear, who is marrying this nation? It is the LORD – and this is no marriage of convenience. Isaiah has made it clear the price He had to pay, and now Isaiah reveals the emotional expression of God – He delights in His bride! (See 62:4.)

Isaiah describes the groom rejoicing over the bride; in the same way, God will rejoice over His people! (62:5) God promises to protect His bride (62:8-9). He has won the battle, paid the price, and so now the people are called by four glorious names (62:12):

The Holy People – God's bride is set apart from all others, clothed in righteousness and honoured with a unique role and purpose.

The Redeemed of the LORD – God's bride has been paid for at the cost of great bloodshed. The Servant of the LORD gave everything.

Sought Out – God's bride was sought out. This means God went to great lengths to find, woo and win His bride. God never said, 'She will do.' Instead God did everything to get this particular bride. Later Jesus would say to His disciples, 'You did not choose me, but I chose you.' (John 15:16)

A City Not Forsaken – God's bride is not abandoned. This is no once-loved wife now left as the husband moves on to new and prettier pursuits. God makes promises and keeps them. God's way of dealing with humanity is through a faithful marital covenant.

Holy, redeemed, sought out, never forsaken. There could be no higher privilege than to be the bride of God Himself!

11 | **The Voice of the Bridegroom**

• JEREMIAH

The seventh century was the greatest moment of impending destruction for the nation; yet in the midst of the faithful warnings of God's servants came one of the most spectacular series of promises of hope.[1]

WALTER C KAISER JR.

It is not thy sinfulness, nor thy base condition, that can hinder it: Christ never joins himself to any because they *are* worthy, but that they *may be* worthy; and he makes them so by the very act of union. The woman is not married to

---

1. Walter C Kaiser Jr., *The Promise Plan of God* (Zondervan, 2008), p. 203.

the king because she is a queen, but the king marries her to
make her a queen.[2]

JEREMIAH BURROUGHS

Judah was heading for disaster. In the decades since the
death of Isaiah, Babylon had become a fierce threat. Now,
more than ever, the clock was ticking for Judah. During the
most tempestuous era of regional political turmoil, Jeremiah
first met the Word of the LORD and then the word of the
LORD rang out clearly from his mouth.

Jeremiah's ministry began in 627 B.C. and continued past
the fall of Jerusalem in 587 B.C. During this time King Josiah
teamed up with him to seek reform after the discovery of the
book of the law of God. Josiah's reform, like Josiah himself,
came to a quick and sad end. Judah was heading for defeat
to the Babylonians. Other prophets overlap with this time
frame, but Jeremiah is the big name, with the longest book –
a blazing torch in the darkest of times.

Not Married

Jeremiah was not married. Unlike other prophets with
spouses, God explicitly told Jeremiah not to marry. The reason
was that He wanted to spare Jeremiah the heartache of seeing
his spouse and children dying in the worst of circumstances.
God had withdrawn His peace from the people and they
were hurting. Jeremiah was not to participate personally in
the mourning. He was to anticipate the sad day when the
dead of Jerusalem would not be mourned. And Jeremiah was
not to participate when there was feasting either, for someday
soon that would also come to an end (16:1-9).

---

2. Jeremiah Burroughs, *An Exposition of Hosea*, p. 161.

Jeremiah's non-participation would raise questions for the people. They would ask why God was pronouncing such evil on them. Jeremiah was to tell them that their fathers had forsaken the LORD, going off after other gods, failing to obey the law. Since this generation was even worse than those that had gone before, they would be expelled from the land to discover what it really meant to serve other gods. (16:10-13)

God was not married either. His wife had turned away and forsaken Him.

Forsaking the Fountain

The book of Jeremiah is not easy to follow if you are looking for chronological progression; section after section seem to come from different moments in his life. But Jeremiah is easy to follow if you are looking at the images he uses. After his call in chapter 1, Jeremiah focuses on the broken covenant and Judah's impending discipline via the Babylonian conquest from chapters 2–29. After this comes the hope of restoration and the new covenant from 30–33. He describes the final days of Jerusalem in his lifetime from chapters 34–45. Finally he offers a block of oracles against the nations from chapters 46–51, and concludes in chapter 52.

Jeremiah launches his book with a stunning salvo of intensely relational material.

> 'I remember the devotion of your youth,
>   your love as a bride,
> how you followed me in the wilderness,
>   in a land not sown.
> Israel was holy to the LORD,
>   the firstfruits of his harvest.' (2:2-3)

God looked back to where it all began. He reminisced about Israel's devotion and love. She was His bride, and she followed Him with such loyalty. She was holy, set apart in love for Him and to Him (although if we look closely at that era, it certainly was not consistent dedication!)

Now God spoke with incredulity. What fault did those ancestors find in Him that led them to forsake Him? Their hearts turned from God and went after worthless things, resulting in their becoming worthless (for we will always reflect what we love). God had done so much for them, but they turned away from Him (2:4-8).

The desertion of God by His people was truly bizarre. But God would not be passive toward them – He would continue to contend with them. He challenged them to go travelling and see if another nation had ever changed their gods. These other nations had good reason to do so, since their gods were not real. Strangely, the other nations didn't forsake their gods, but Israel had turned from hers (2:9-11).

Israel had committed two great evils. First, she had turned away from the fountain of living waters. Imagine the wonder of having pure, fresh, cold, clean water pouring forth with extravagant abundance in a hot Middle Eastern country. Nothing could be more luxurious. Israel had that, in her God, and yet had turned away.

Second, she started to dig an alternative water facility. She chiseled her way into the rock, piece by piece, chip by chip. Gradually this new cistern took shape. In the heat of the sun, facing the challenge of carving into solid rock, she gave herself to her task. She sweated. She strived. She pressed on until a cistern was formed. Now she didn't need the fountain anymore, just a quick rain shower and she would be independently watered! So the rain came, and the water entered, and she found the cistern was compromised by a crack – it would hold no water!

Why would God's people ever be unfaithful to Him? Why turn from a life-giving fountain and give oneself to digging a useless alternative? This is a question we should all ask ourselves at various times in our lives. Why do we turn from our faithful God and look for satisfaction elsewhere?

So Jeremiah continues to speak of the evil of forsaking God. By the way, he loves to use the word 'to turn' – they had turned from God (forsaken), but they were being called to turn back to God.

They had broken free of their bond to God, refusing to serve Him. Yet 'on every high hill and under every green tree' they bowed down, 'like a whore.' (2:20) Notice how their desire for independence had led only to slavery elsewhere. Sin is always that way; it promises freedom and gives nothing of the sort. Notice Israel's full exploration of all that the surrounding nations had to offer – on *every* high hill and under *every* green tree. Israel abandoned herself to her whoring.

They were planted as a choice vine, but became a wild vine. They washed themselves with soap, but the dirt remained. They were pure, but became a restless young camel, or a donkey on heat, unrestrained in her lust and desperate to go after foreigners for further liaisons (2:20-25).

Israel had turned her back on God and treated trees as her father, and stones as her mother. Yet when trouble came along, the people of Israel would still call on God to get involved. So God asked, sarcastically, that they let the new gods arise and do some saving … if they can! (2:26-28)

The marital theme is strong throughout this section. God is amazed that while a virgin cannot forget her ornaments, nor a bride her wedding dress, God's people have forgotten Him! (2:32)

Divorced, Forever?

Chapter 3 continues the marital theme with a shocking insight. God points to the divorce laws in Deuteronomy 24:1-4 and asks if there is provision for remarriage to a divorced spouse who has gone off and remarried? There is no provision for that kind of remarriage. But Israel had been a whore to numerous other lovers. How could there be any return to God? Under the provisions of the law, there really was no way back (Jer. 3:1).

It seems that Israel was unaware of how serious her sin was before God. So God pointed to the various hills around – where hadn't they been unfaithful? There were fully utilised idol stations everywhere! Israel had been like the cheapest of prostitutes, propositioning lovers in the easiest of pick-up locations. Israel had been like an unfaithful spouse who has used every hotel room in town. Yet she expected God to ignore all that and be kind to her! (Jer. 3:2-5)

So God summarised the situation in 3:6-10 – Judah (the southern kingdom) saw Israel's (the northern kingdom's) whoring, as well as God's decree of divorce (the Assyrian defeat of Israel), and yet she still copied Israel and did the same things. When she did return to God, it was only in pretence, not wholeheartedly. So God called out to Israel to turn back and trust in His mercy (3:11-14). He would provide shepherds after His own heart, who would lead the people to fruitfulness and understanding. Despite what the law said, their forsaking of God, their husband, did not mean there was no way back. He wanted them back. His arms were open to this treacherous wife (3:20); He was ready to heal their faithlessness (3:22 – literally here He writes, 'turn back, O turning-away Son, and I will heal your turn-iness').

They had tasted and discovered the vacuous emptiness of exploring reckless abandon in spiritual orgies on the mountains. Truly it is only in the LORD God that there is salvation (3:23).

God doesn't raise the subject of divorce lightly here. He shows how there is no provision in the law for restoration after there has been a divorce and remarriage to another. Yet He will restore Judah to Himself. God's steadfast love is truly astonishing.

But to get a full sense of God's view of divorce in the Old Testament, we would also need to pop over to Malachi 2:10-16. There we find the prophet after the exile rebuking the people of Israel for their covenant unfaithfulness. They were unfaithful vertically, with God, and horizontally, with their own spouses. God had united them with their spouses, binding them together by the Spirit and seeking godly offspring. Bottom line? ' "I hate divorce," says the LORD God of Israel.' (2:16 NASB)

Back in Jeremiah, the theme of Judah's disgusting and lustful harlotry comes up again in 5:7-8 and 13:25-27, but there is another marital motif that is repeated poignantly in Jeremiah:

The Joy Not Heard

God wanted the nation to know how serious He was. Three times He repeats the ultimate description of joy removed:

> And I will silence in the cities of Judah and in the streets of Jerusalem the voice of mirth and the voice of gladness, the voice of the bridegroom and the voice of the bride, for the land shall become a waste. (7:34)

127

Jeremiah describes a coming time of slaughter, but the ultimate feature is the ending of weddings. No more joyous celebration. We are wired for relationship, so our greatest joys and our greatest agony will always come in the context of relationship or relational failure.

Again in 16:9 God repeats His plan to silence and end the wedding celebrations. The reason is requested and given – because they turned from God and went after other gods. Weddings just don't seem appropriate any more after such gross spiritual immorality and adultery.

Again in 25:10, as Jeremiah reaches the climax of his anticipation of judgment, he repeats that the voice of the bridegroom and bride will be silenced. The nation had forsaken the LORD and the time had come for judgment at the hands of Babylon.

Jeremiah was known as the weeping prophet. For one thing, he gave more insight into his own biographical situation and struggles than any other prophet. For another, his shocking message didn't seem to touch the veneer of Judah's unfaithful resolve. But it was not all bad news. There was hope, the greatest hope!

It Will Be Heard Again!

Jeremiah's book of consolation stretches for four chapters, from chapters 30–33. This is a section describing, defining, illustrating and reaffirming God's plan to restore the nation. Consider these words:

> [10] 'Thus says the LORD: In this place of which you say, "It is a waste without man or beast," in the cities of Judah and the streets of Jerusalem that are desolate, without man or inhabitant or beast, there shall be heard again [11] the voice of

mirth and the voice of gladness, the voice of the bridegroom and the voice of the bride, the voices of those who sing, as they bring thank offerings to the house of the Lord':

> '"Give thanks to the Lord of hosts,
>> for the Lord is good,
>>> for his steadfast love endures forever!
>
> For I will restore the fortunes of the land as at first,"
> says the Lord.' (33:10-11)

The joy of wedding celebration will be heard again! How is this possible?

Chapter 30 – Because God intended to do something new with His people. He would bring them back to the land, judging the nations, but disciplining His own people. The lovers they had lusted after will abandon them (30:14), so through a great upheaval, God would restore His people to their land. Again, they will be His people, and He will be their God (30:22).

Chapter 31 – Jeremiah dreamed a happy dream. Indeed, the Lord will be their God, and they will be His people. Why? Because the Lord has loved Israel with an everlasting love; He has remained faithful (31:3). The harlot is called a virgin again (31:4). God will bring the people home from all over the earth and they will rejoice and dance, their mourning turned to joy, their sorrow exchanged for gladness (31:13-14). God's plan for His people is to make a new covenant with them (31:31-34) – He had been their husband before, but that covenant had been broken. Now He planned a new covenant: the law would be written on their hearts; they would have personal intimacy with God;

129

their sins would be forgiven and remembered no more. What's more, this new covenant would be permanent and unbreakable …not dependent on their obedience, but determined by the trustworthiness of God's Word.

Chapter 32 – In this chapter Jeremiah illustrates what he has been describing. In the midst of the Babylonian siege, he buys a field and then takes the deed to make a public statement – God is making the point that this kind of transaction will be done again in the future, and so He asks Jeremiah to keep this deed safely stored. Jeremiah then prays to God, who answers with a description of His plan – short term with their exile to Babylon, and longer term with the return of His people to their land. They will be God's people and He will be their God (32:38). He will make an everlasting covenant with them, doing a transformative work in their hearts (32:40).

Chapter 33 – Babylon was about to destroy the city as part of God's plan, but ultimately God planned to restore their fortunes and rebuild their city. In the process their guilt would be cleansed and forgiven. Wedding celebrations would be heard in the city again! How would all this happen? By the righteous Branch Himself, the Messiah (also described in Jeremiah 23:5), who would execute justice and righteousness. The LORD Himself would be the righteousness of this desperately unrighteous people.

Truly Jeremiah 30–33 should bring tears to the eyes of God's people – the weeping prophet stirs wonderful hope here in the darkest of days for Judah.

Unresponsive Hearts

God had been abandoned by His people. They had bruised His heart, and rejected His messenger Jeremiah. The word of the LORD through Jeremiah had tried to provoke the hearts of the people, stirring them to see who they were and what evil they had done. It was all to no avail. As Babylon took Judah into exile, Jeremiah handed over to Ezekiel the prophetic baton of shocking whoredom imagery, and stunning New Covenant hope – perhaps Ezekiel could stir a response.

12   Will Anything Shock Her?

• EZEKIEL

Christ has brought it to pass, that those who the Father has given to him should be brought into the household of God, that he and his Father and they should be as it were one society of the three persons in the Godhead. In this family or household God [is] the Father, Jesus Christ is his own naturally and eternally begotten Son. The saints, they also are children in the family; the church is the daughter of God, being the spouse of his Son. They all have communion in the same Spirit, the Holy Ghost.[1]

JONATHAN EDWARDS

1. Jonathan Edwards, *Miscellanies (No.571),* in *The Works of Jonathan Edwards,* vol. 18 (New Haven, CT: Yale University Press, 1957–2009), p. 110.

Come, Almighty to deliver,
let us all thy life receive;
suddenly return and never,
nevermore thy temples leave.
Thee we would be always blessing,
serve thee as thy hosts above,
pray and praise thee without ceasing,
glory in thy perfect love.[2]

CHARLES WESLEY
Love Divine, All Loves Excelling

Jeremiah and Ezekiel lived at the same time, but far from each other. Ezekiel was taken to Babylon in an early deportation and so ministered to the Jewish people there while Jeremiah was coming to the end of his career back home. Ezekiel was called to speak to the people of God in Babylon and point them to God. He spoke compellingly of the sovereignty and glory of the LORD, declaring seventy times in his book, 'then you will know that I am the LORD.' The people needed to be reassured that God was very much on the throne, despite what their circumstances might suggest.

The God portrayed by Ezekiel is not just out there somewhere, on His throne. He is also a God who wants to dwell in the midst of His people. The presence of the LORD is a great theme that holds the book together. In the first section, chapters 1–24, the focus is on the sad and poignant departure of the presence of the LORD from the temple and from Jerusalem. God wanted to remain, but the shocking unfaithfulness of the people had reached horrific heights.

2. Charles Wesley, 'Love Divine, All Loves Excelling,' Hymn, 1747.

After the middle section, declaring God's sovereignty over the nations surrounding Judah, the final section from chapters 33–48 is all about the return of God's presence to be in the midst of His people. He will restore them, give them new hearts, bring them alive spiritually, and re-establish true worship in the city. The final verse of the entire book points to the name of the city from that time on, 'Yahweh Shammah' – The LORD is there! (Ezek. 48:35).

Interestingly, Ezekiel is the third prophet we have considered whose own marriage played into his ministry directly. Jeremiah was told not to marry since so much death was coming and God did not want him in mourning. Singleness is tough. Hosea had been told to marry a wife who would become a prostitute and leave him. Infidelity is tough. Ezekiel was married but his wife dies as Jerusalem is under siege. Bereavement is tough.

The siege of Jerusalem in chapter 24 concludes the first part of Ezekiel's book. The word of the LORD came to Ezekiel and told him that 'the delight of his eyes' would be taken away at a stroke, but he was not to mourn or weep in order to act out the heartlessness of the people. (See 24:15-27.) Ezekiel was bereaved of his wife, just as God was about to be 'bereaved' of His.

How did it get to this point for God's people? Just in case Jeremiah did not explain the situation sufficiently, perhaps Ezekiel could take the infidelity example that Jeremiah used and play it out in more detail for us.

She Never Left the Field – Chapter 16

Jerusalem was far from God and didn't seem to grasp the seriousness of her situation. So the word of the LORD came to Ezekiel to make known to the city her abominations (v. 2).

135

In this story Jerusalem is personified with stunning effect. Ezekiel is going to tell Jerusalem her life story. She was born to pagan parents who did not want her. After her birth she was abandoned with her afterbirth in an open field to die from exposure (vv. 2-5).

God passed by and saw her wallowing in her blood. He gave her life and she flourished, becoming a fully developed and beautiful young lady. God passed by again and invited her into holy matrimony. He made His vow to her and she became His. He cared for her and gave her jewellery and clothing, as well as good food. She grew and became resplendent and regal. This was God's chosen bride, the Queen famed worldwide for her beauty (vv. 6-14).

The wonderful story suddenly turns desperately sour. She trusted in her beauty and proceeded to give it away to others who had no right to it. She took the beautiful clothing given to her by God and made tools of the trade for her new vocation. She used her God-given incense to set the mood. She took the food God gave and turned it into a potpourri to make her little sexual altar smell good. And just to show how bad things were, she took the children God had given her and sacrificed them to a foreign god. And through it all, she did not recall how her life had begun (vv. 15-22).

Remember, Ezekiel is describing the idolatry of Jerusalem, which is spiritual adultery, as if it were literal prostitution. This chapter is so gripping that it feels like that is what actually happened. The moment we realise it is a description of sacrificing to idols we can feel slightly detached from the nonsense of giving gifts to little statues. However, worshipping idols is just one way of projecting our natural desires into our life. How easily do we give God's gracious gifts to us away to the flesh-projections of our native culture?

'Their conduct in this was simply an example of the native effect of the world upon the heart, according to the circumstances of the time; and when our Lord, speaking for all times, sets before us the prodigal son, selfishly coveting his portion of goods, and going to spend them in alienation from his father's house, he but presents us with another exhibition, differently modified, of the same great truth. Let the heart of nature be fed to the full with gifts, and there will never fail to appear, in one form or another, the idolatry of self and the world.'[3]

So God, her husband, is already deeply hurt and angered by this stage, but it only gets worse. Next, she builds love shacks in every town square (easy access for her companions). She selected the busy places so that picking up men would be easy. This probably represents the pervasiveness of idol altars in Judah. She even went and gave herself to the Egyptians, presumably a reference to illegitimate foreign alliances, thus provoking God to still greater anger. Then she went to the Assyrians, playing the whore for every man and every nation that came by. Babylon too. Israel was never sated by these illicit affairs with other nations (vv. 23-29).

'How sick is your heart, declares the Lord GOD, because you did all these things, the deeds of a brazen prostitute,' building love shacks all over the place. In fact, just to make things worse, she even refused payment. In fact, she went and paid her lovers to come to her! Israel was a loved wife whose husband had in no way failed her, but she wanted the adultery for its own sake, just for the thrill. (vv. 30-34)

---

3. Patrick Fairbairn, *Exposition of Ezekiel,* (Edinburgh: T&T Clark, 1855, reprint 1960), p. 170.

God is so angered that now He is going to act. He is going to bring together all her lovers and shame her before them. Naked and shamed is not so attractive as scantily clad. Naked and shamed is where she started. Naked and shamed is where she chose to return. So she will be judged … surprisingly, by her many lovers. They will want nothing more of her and will delight to rain down judgment on her as they plunder the land and take her into captivity (vv. 35-43).

So all people will speak of her with a proverb: like mother, like daughter. Her family background makes sense of all this. Her older sister, Samaria, the capital of the northern kingdom, and her younger sister, Sodom, to the south, were both bad too. But Jerusalem, who was the most privileged, was the worst! (vv. 44-52)

Writing these next two words never grows old: 'but God …' In this case, despite all the shocking infidelity of His people, God still remains determined to care for them. So He will restore. He will restore Samaria, and Sodom, and even Jerusalem (vv. 53-58).

And what is the nature of that restoration? It is marriage, and it is by covenant (this time, an everlasting one!) God will make Himself known, and make Jerusalem His bride once more. The shamed city will remember her sin, but she will never be shamed again! (vv. 59-63)

Two Sisters – Ezekiel 23

The powerful imagery of chapter 16 returns again in chapter 23. This time God picks up the idea of the two sisters, Samaria and Jerusalem (the capitals of the northern and southern kingdoms). Immediately He describes them playing the whore in their youth, while in Egypt. But they became His. Samaria is given the name, Oholah. Jerusalem, for this tale, is dubbed Oholibah. This passage is not suggesting that the LORD was a polygamist. Israel was one nation birthed out of Egypt, but by the time Ezekiel spoke, the nation was divided into two, He addressed one of two nations. In this passage He will be speaking to only one of these nations, but He will be contrasting the two, hence the need for two sisters in this tale of Israel's relational history (vv. 1-4).

What is the significance of the two names? Oholah and Oholibah are obviously closely connected – just as Samaria and Jerusalem were historically. However, there is a subtle difference. Oholah means 'she has her own tent' and stands for Samaria – whose worship of the LORD centred around the two golden calves. Oholibah means 'my tent is in her' and speaks of Jerusalem being the legitimate worship centre for the LORD. Ultimately it is this greater privilege that will mean Jerusalem's spiritual adultery is evaluated as the more serious of the two.

Oholah was smitten with the Assyrian soldiers – she wanted them. She never learned. She never pulled back from her idolatrous whoring and so God gave her what she wanted with reality mixed in. Assyria came and plundered Israel. Ray Ortlund puts it in graphic terms fitting with the text: 'The very ones Oholah lusted after did come to her, but with violent intent. One envisions a breathless Oholah awaiting her sexy Assyrian boyfriends, only to be raped by them when they arrive. Tragic, gullible Israel – now the topic of ridicule among the nations.'[4] (vv. 5-10)

Next Ezekiel comes to his own audience, Oholibah. Surely the younger sister would learn from seeing what happened to her older sister? Actually, no. She surpassed

---

4. Ray Ortlund, Jr., *God's Unfaithful Wife,* 1996, p. 122.

her sibling in moral degradation. First, she replicated her sister's falling for the impressive pomp of the Assyrian army. Judah flirted with Assyria; instead of trusting God, she had tried to form alliances. But it got worse. Oholibah saw pictures of the Chaldeans (the Babylonians) and lusted after them, coming together in political summit; since this was about securing her future, this too was spiritual adultery. She was unsatisfied by the tryst with Babylon, but instead of turning to God, Oholibah looked back on the idolatry and affiliations of her youth in Egypt. Now Ezekiel's language gets extreme – 'she ... lusted after her lovers there, whose members were like those of donkeys and whose issue was like that of horses. Thus you longed for the lewdness of your youth, when the Egyptians handled your bosom and pressed your young breasts.' (vv. 20-21) Ezekiel 23 should turn the stomach of God's people as we read it. He was trying to get them to wake up to their desperate situation! (vv. 11-21)

So what is to happen to privileged but straying Oholibah? All the soldiers she desired are coming against her as the fury of her husband's jealousy. This is what it would take to bring an end to the lewd whoring that had always been her story. The particular nation who disgusted her before, Babylon, will be the one who comes and strips naked this girl who so wanted to flaunt herself to them. (vv. 22-35)

Ezekiel, the prophet with a priestly background, is now brought on stage to evaluate the sisters. They had committed adultery with idols, even offering their children in sacrifice. They had committed this sin against God while continuing an outward form of Yahweh worship – like an adulterous wife coming home after her liaisons to pretend she is faithful. Yet the pretence was so shallow, for these sisters openly invited men from abroad – like putting personal ads in the press? – and openly partied with those who came, showering gifts on them (vv. 36-42).

Finally God looks on the wasted wreck of His wife. He predicts that the same men who came as emissaries from foreign powers shall come with the power of judgment against God's people. The future looks extremely bleak at this point. This chapter is the strongest possible warning: God will put an end to the lewd harlotry of Judah. They will know that He is the Lord GOD (vv. 43-49).

What Next?

It is at this point in the text of Ezekiel that God tells His prophet that the siege has begun. It is at this point that Ezekiel's wife dies, but he is not to mourn as another shocking means of communicating God's message to the people. God has truly lost His wife, and Ezekiel 23 tells the story so all can understand why. Is that it? Is God's great covenant of marriage with His people at an end?

Just a few chapters later, the last section of Ezekiel stirs great hope. God will make a covenant with Judah again (see 34:25). He takes the initiative to restore honour to His name and regather His people in Israel again. He will sprinkle them clean – clean from all their uncleanness, clean from all their idolatry. He will give them a new heart, and put a new spirit in them, and their hard hearts will be replaced with sensitive, beating hearts of love for God. They will be careful to obey Him, they will dwell in the land once more (see 36:22-36). He will not only put them back in their land, but He will put His own sanctuary in their midst again; He will dwell with His people. He will be their God and they will be His people! (See 37:21-28; 48:35.)

The latter section of Ezekiel is heart stirring, just as the latter section of Isaiah had been. The prophets pointed forward and offered hope beyond the failure. With our Spirit-sensitised hearts, the prophets can have a greater impact in our lives than they had in their ministry to the people of Israel and Judah.

Ultimately the hope of marital covenant between God and man culminates not in the powerful images and shocking language used by the prophets, but with the arrival of the groom Himself. So let us fast forward a few centuries and cross over into the era of the New Covenant. Here comes the groom!

Part Three

Here Comes the Groom

Whence is it that we are 'sons of God'? Because he was the 'Son of man,' 'God in our flesh.' … God became man that man might be one with God; God was 'manifested in the flesh,' that we might be united to him; and being brought again to God the Father, we might come again to a glorious union.[1]

RICHARD SIBBES

---

1. Richard Sibbes, *Fountains Opened,* in Works, vol. 5 (Edinburgh, Banner of Truth, 1973), p. 479.

13 Jesus: Union Personified ... Birth

• GOD AND MAN

We must understand that as long as Christ remains outside of us, and we are separated from him, all that he has suffered and done for the salvation of the human race remains useless and of no value to us. Therefore, to share in what he has received from the Father, he had to become ours and to dwell with us ... for, as I have said, all that he possesses is nothing to us until we grow into one body with him.[1]

JOHN CALVIN

---

1. John Calvin, *Institutes of the Christian Religion*, ed. John T. McNeil, trans. Ford Lewis Battles, Library of Christian Classics, Vols. 20–21 (Philadelphia: Westminster, 1960), Book 3, chapter 1, paragraph 1.

Christ by highest heaven adored
Christ the everlasting Lord
Late in time behold him come,
Offspring of a virgin's womb.
Veiled in flesh the Godhead see;
Hail, the incarnate deity,
Pleased as man with man to dwell
Jesus, our Emmanuel!
Hark! the herald angels sing,
Glory to the newborn King.[2]

CHARLES WESLEY
Hark the Herald Angels Sing

A blank page in our Bibles covers a lot of history. Not only the rise and fall of world empires, but also generations of silence in Israel. Actually, things have seldom been silent in Israel, but for a people whose history is so rich with prophetic revelation, the centuries of heavenly silence after Malachi must have felt eerily quiet.

Following the Babylonian captivity, the Gentile oppression of Israel continued with the Persians, who then gave way to the Greeks. The Greek culture was then mixed into the strong rule of Rome. During those centuries Israel experienced nationalistic fights for freedom as well as some religious transition with the synagogue system becoming established. But through it all, hope for the longed-for Messiah remained a feature of national, cultural and religious anticipation.

Would the Messiah be a freedom fighter, taking up the sword to throw off the oppressive Roman occupation? Would He be a religious recluse, leading the devoted to higher

---

2. Charles Wesley, 'Hark the Herald Angels Sing', Hymn, 1739.

levels of spiritual enlightenment? Would He be a political mastermind, negotiating His way to power in a complex and politically charged world? As the blank page gives way to the Gospels we find the answer is a resounding *No*! to all of these Messianic profiles. The Messiah was better than the Jews had ever imagined!

The Messiah Came to Create the Great Union

Matthew launches his Gospel with a carefully shaped, land-marked and unlikely genealogy. The shape is seen in the number of generations he lists. The landmarks are the key moments in Israel's history when God gave His promise to the nation: to Abraham, to David, and through the prophets in the New Covenant around the time of the exile. Now the fulfilment of God's promise was about to arrive on the scene. The unlikely element of the genealogy turns out to be central to all that would follow in the story of the birth of Jesus.

God had promised to bless all the families of the earth through the seed of Abraham. God had promised to give a forever kingdom to the coming seed in the line of David. In the New Covenant, God had promised to forgive sins, transform hearts and give His Spirit for the sake of intimate union between humans and Himself. The promised Seed, the Blesser, the King, the Forgiver, the Heart-Winner, yes, the Groom, was now entering the world!

If our anticipation levels are not sky high when we pass the blank page into the New Testament, then it is tempting to suggest that we need to read the Old Testament again. So many great themes of the Scripture converge in the arrival of Jesus that we should be struggling to hold the pages still enough to read them. So much anticipation, but His arrival was as unlikely as could ever have been imagined.

Before we leave the genealogy, is it fair to call it 'unlikely?' Absolutely. Yes it begins with Abraham and features David, but it also contains some unlikely characters, not least the women who are listed. The fact that women are named is itself unusual in the extreme, but amazingly the ladies chosen aren't exactly pristine in their reputation. There was Tamar who acted as a shrine prostitute to get pregnant by her father-in-law. There was Rahab who didn't act as a prostitute, she really was one. There was righteous Ruth who followed her mother-in-law's plan to proposition a drunk landowner under his blanket in the middle of the night. There was Bathsheba, the wife of a loyal soldier who became pregnant by the king in an illicit tryst. And there was Mary who was pregnant because God bypassed her virginity and gave her a son – or so she said.

The Messiah was born to a young and unmarried girl who was hardly a likely candidate for such a key role. Mary was probably a young teen. She had grown up in the unlikely town of Nazareth and was engaged to be married to the young town carpenter, Joseph. Nazareth was a rest stop on the way to somewhere better. Nobody would wear a Nazareth t-shirt with pride. If anything was unlikely, it was a virgin in Nazareth. Mary was one. But she was pregnant. It was more than a little awkward.

Mary had been visited by an angel who reassured her and let her know that God was at work in her life. Her response was one of great trust, but would others trust her word if she explained why she was growing at the waistline? Not a chance.

Joseph had also been visited by an angel to give him the necessary explanation. He also responded with impressive faith, but would others trust his word if he explained how his not-yet-wife was looking very wife-like? No way.

Everyone assumed that the 'virgin' was not and that the trustworthy carpenter was either a liar or a fool. These were hardly the best circumstances to launch their married life. Perhaps the required trip to Bethlehem was a welcome excuse to get out of town as tongues wagged and rumours spread.

So Mary was with Joseph, staying in Bethlehem when it came time to deliver her special bundle. The combination of pain and fatigue, anticipation and doubts, all culminated as the little boy spluttered His first cry (in a human body). It is hard to imagine what Mary felt and thought as she held Him close and looked into His eyes. Could she grasp that this was the Messiah, the promised deliverer, the anticipated ruler, the fulfilment of God's plans, and the precious son of the Most High? Somehow this little one would bring blessing to all the families of the earth, rule the world, and transform hearts for close fellowship with God in heaven.

How could one so small forge the greatest union – uniting a recalcitrant and rebellious humanity with a holy and glorious God?

We think we have some idea of how Jesus could forge a union between God and humanity, but we struggle to get our heads around the union that was forged in Him. For the next few centuries theologians would debate the nature of the union that is Christ. For Mary, the situation was reversed: she didn't understand how love had drawn salvation's plan, but in some way she understood the union that was her son.

The Messiah Came as a Great Union

Jesus was human. She had felt Him grow, she had already begun to love Him even before she saw the elbows that rippled her bulging womb. His cry, His tears, His eager nursing, His tired sighs. Jesus was human. Jesus was her little boy.

Jesus was divine. Mary the virgin had miraculously conceived as the Spirit of God established the life within her womb. Mary had seen and heard the angel who brought the greatest news of glad tidings to her those months before. And despite what everybody said or thought, Mary knew that only God could have launched this life she now held.

Mary would not have been able to define the hypostatic union of two natures in one person: fully God, fully man, fully one. Mary was not studying theology; she was just holding the Son of God. Even without the vocabulary, she must have known.

Every little baby boy has the potential to grow up to be a groom one day. This baby boy produced the possibility of a marriage by His very nature. In order for the glorious union that is the Trinity to one day unite in marriage with a redeemed humanity there was a door that needed to open … someone had to establish a point of connection between humanity and God. Jesus did not just come to achieve salvation by what He would do, He also came to provide a way for a special kind of salvation by virtue of who He was.

Perhaps God could have orchestrated a way to overcome our guilt, wipe our records clean and offer us a heavenly pardon from a distance. But to make possible a wedding between God's Son and humanity, God's Son first had to become one of us. The great divide was bridged, not only at Easter, but in a preliminary way, at Christmas. God and humanity became one, so that some day God and redeemed humanity could be truly one.

Where Heaven and Earth Meet

Maybe Mary was lost in Jesus' little eyes or cries as she cradled her newborn son. But any heavenly activity camera would have spotted the splash made in the very earthy surroundings of His birth. Nearby there were some shepherds. Hardly a career in the city, shepherding was gritty work. A group of poor men going about their business in the fields when suddenly heaven broke into their world and lit up the night sky. Forget the nativity plays with little children dressed in modified bed sheets; the real scene would have been breathtaking. When heaven bursts in, it should rock our worlds and take our breath away. Can you imagine a heavenly chorus bursting forth in praise? We can only try.

The shepherds knew where to go looking for the new baby – they knew where a feeding trough would be. So they came. The poor. The insignificant. The marginalised. They came to a poor, young, engaged couple in a poor town.

When heaven breaks in, normal life gets turned upside down. Traditional nativity scenes bring together some lowly shepherds with a strange group of foreign dignitaries. It has become almost as traditional to point out that these 'wise men' probably arrived quite a bit later since the text tells us they came to the house (and we all know the shepherds came to the cow shed). Actually, Jesus was probably not born in a cow shed, but in the living room of a poor family. The Bible tells us about the manger, not the shed, and the manger would have probably been in the home since in those days, the animals were brought in at night to keep them safe and the house warm. The Bible tells us not about a hotel, but about a guest room already full, which would have meant that guests would have stayed in the family's living quarters, where the manger was, in the house. So maybe the shepherds and wise men did all converge that night.

A group of shepherds, the lowest locals on any social ladder. A group of foreign dignitaries, mysterious, bearing expensive gifts Mary would never have received at home, even if she was given a baby shower. The richest and the most powerful people this young couple had probably ever met, alongside the type of common folk these dignitaries would probably have never acknowledged. Rich and poor. Jewish and Gentile. The elite and the ignored. Brought together by this little boy. He was only a few hours old and He was already bringing people together.[3]

Religion has a bad rap for dividing people, but history also tells of the uniquely effective uniting power of Jesus. The most unlikely of combinations are found under the name of this Jesus – enemies reconciled, offender and victim embracing, class strata overcome, skin colour ignored, all because of Jesus. But the greatest union that Christmas night was not shepherds and wise men, even though that was an impressive glimpse of things to come. The greatest union in that room was Jesus Himself – fully God, fully man, fully one. And that made possible what was to come – His future marriage union to His bride who is made up of diverse humanity united together – humanity united to God, in union with Him.

---

3. For more on the timing of this event, see Peter Mead, *Pleased To Dwell* (Christian Focus: 2014), p. 93.

14 **Jesus the Wedding Storyteller**

• VARIOUS

So the saints are said to live by Christ living in them
(Gal. 2:20). Christ by his Spirit not only is in them, but
lives in them ... The Spirit of God so dwells in the hearts of
the saints, that he there, as a seed or spring of life, exerts and
communicates himself, in this his sweet and divine nature,
making the soul a partaker of God's beauty and Christ's
joy, so that the saint has truly fellowship with the Father,
and with his Son Jesus Christ, in thus having communion
or participation of the Holy Ghost.[1]

JONATHAN EDWARDS

---

1. Jonathan Edwards, 'Religious Affections', *Works*, vol. 2 (Yale, 2009),
   p. 200–201.

Thou, O Christ, art all I want;
   More than all in Thee I find:
Raise the fallen, cheer the faint,
   Heal the sick, and lead the blind.
Just and holy is Thy name;
   I am all unrighteousness:
False and full of sin I am;
   Thou art full of truth and grace.

Plenteous grace with Thee is found,
   Grace to cover all my sin;
Let the healing streams abound,
   Make and keep me pure within.
Thou of life the fountain art
   Freely let me take of Thee:
Spring Thou up within my heart,
   Rise to all eternity![2]

CHARLES WESLEY
Jesus, Lover of My Soul

For a single man, Jesus talked quite a bit about weddings. For instance, on His way to the showdown with the authorities in Jerusalem, Jesus gave a wedding parable to some guests at a meal. It was a Sabbath, of course. It is amazing how many times Jesus chose the Sabbath to court controversy with the religious elite! Jesus had been invited to be a guest at the house of a ruler of the Pharisees. He could tell He was being watched carefully. So when a man with a disability presented the opportunity, Jesus asked whether these guests, this jury of religious evaluators, would see it as lawful to heal a man on the Sabbath. Blank stares gave way to stumped silence as

---

2. Charles Wesley, 'Jesus Lover of My Soul', Hymn, 1740.

Jesus healed the man and rebuked their inconsistency (after all, they would rescue an animal on a Sabbath!)

So He told them a parable about a wedding. It was a helpful life lesson, but with an in-built rebuke. When you are invited to a wedding feast, sit at the lowest table so that you get moved up toward the top table. Don't aim high and get brought down with a bump. Humble yourself and get exalted, not vice versa. Simple story. But surely it was a rebuke too. After all, Jesus told this story while He was at a meal with the social elite. Was He suggesting they were full of themselves? Was He suggesting they should move down and away from the top table? Was this one in their company too significant for them? (Luke 14:1-11)

On this occasion He immediately added another parable about a banquet and reinforced the rebuke of the elite at the table. The parable tells how the invited elite rejected the invitation to the wedding, and how the master decided to urge the riff-raff in to take the key places. Riff-raff, that is, the kind of people Jesus liked to hang out with normally, the ones He would heal out of compassion for their needs. (Luke 14:12-24)

The Marriage Conundrum

Once Jesus arrived in Jerusalem, the authorities wanted to trap Him in His own words. They failed. First, the Pharisees sent some of their disciples to tag team with some Herodians to find out if Jesus would side with Rome or with Israel in the great tax debate. Jesus sided with God. Round one to Jesus. (See Matt. 22:15-22.)

Next came the Sadducees. Ding Ding, round two! The gospels helpfully explain that they didn't believe in a future resurrection. Actually they didn't affirm the books of the

Bible beyond those attributed to Moses, nor did they believe in angels. So they posed what they thought was a ridiculous question. The Sadducees painted a complicated picture: Suppose a man marries his dead older brother's wife in order to fulfil the expectation under the Old Testament system of levirate marriage but later dies himself. Suppose more brothers keep marrying her but dying, and in the end seven of them have married this woman. Whose wife will she be in the next life? Good question, is Jesus now on the ropes? Not exactly.

Jesus' answer is a genius comeback with a crowd-pleasing sucker punch, so to speak, for good measure. He rebuked their lack of knowledge of the Bible and of God's power. 'For in the resurrection they neither marry nor are given in marriage, but are like angels in heaven.' (Matt. 22:30) Cue crowd laughter. Jesus denied the complexity of the question with an answer about heaven, with an added quip about angels both of which the Sadducees didn't believe in! (I wonder if He gave a playful smile to the crowds nearby?) And with the crowd laughing, Jesus finished off the Sadducees with a quick quote from the part of the Bible they did believe, showing that God is the present-tense God of men who are past-tense from a human perspective.

The Pharisees then came storming in with a bit of a weak question. Umm, Jesus, so which is the greatest commandment in the Law? Huh? Huh? He swiftly dispatched that strategy with a love-God-love-neighbour one-two and then a question about David's Lord in Psalm 110 that left them on the canvas. Unanimous victory.

So back to the poor family of brothers that married the bad cook. Why is it, if the Bible is so pro-marriage, and Jesus is so into the subject, and so much of His teaching seems to point to a future heavenly wedding, that He answered the Sadducees with an apparently anti-marriage comment?

Some do take Jesus' point to mean that there will be no marriage in heaven. My wife and I were disappointed when we heard that because we like being married to each other. Technically, of course, Jesus said there won't be *giving* in marriage. So does that mean our marriages remain? If this is true then quite a few singles will lament that they will have to experience singleness forever (and maybe some married folks will make a comment or two as well!). And if this is true, then the question still stands: who is the forever husband to Mrs Dangerfood or to others who have been married more than once?

Perhaps the point is not that our on-earth status will be frozen, nor that there will be no marriage at all, but perhaps that there will be an overarching, all-consuming, totally thrilling marriage to come. Maybe the earthly experience of marriage is only a glimpse of what lies ahead. Perhaps, whether we are happily married or not, in the future life we will all be fully and totally thrilled with the divine marriage that is to come, so that the brothers won't be fighting for (or against) their status as 4th Mr Dangerfood. (My wife and I are happy to trust God with the issue of our marriage in heaven, but we have requested at least adjoining rooms so that we can hang out together for eternity – knowing God, I suspect that won't be a problem!) (See also Mark 12:18-27 and Luke 20:27-40.)

The Marriage to Come?

Before Jesus got dragged into the various rounds of tension with the local authorities, the chapter began with another wedding parable. Again, this was told as a follow-up to another one that spoke of the authorities' rejection of Jesus (see Matt. 21:33-46 – the parable of the tenants).

Jesus compared the kingdom of heaven to a king giving a wedding feast for his son. Who could this be about? Heaven, a king, his son, a wedding. We probably do not need to hire a theological detective to work it out. Anyway, there were invited guests, but they wouldn't come. So the king sent other servants to try and persuade them, but they still wouldn't come. The servants were killed for trying! So the king sent troops and destroyed the murderers and burned their city. He was the king, after all. So who would come to the wedding of the son of the king? The answer was whatever people the next batch of servants could gather in from the roads.

So is Jesus saying that the city that rejected the prophets was going to be destroyed? That would make sense. And that the invited guests, the religious leadership, would also be destroyed? That too makes sense. And that God's work on the wedding feast won't be wasted? Yes, makes sense again. So therefore both bad and good folks get to be there? That is what it says. But does this make sense? Jesus added a couple more verses to clarify and finishes the story with warning. The king came and looked at the guests, finding one without a wedding garment. Here was one who had sneaked in without appropriately given attire who was thus ejected into outer darkness. Jesus gave it a punchline: many are called, but few are chosen.

The Groom is Here!

One thing that seems certain in the gospels is that Jesus is going to ruffle the feathers of the religious leadership. That is probably why so much action occurs on the Sabbath.

Right after He called Matthew to be His disciple we read about Jesus hanging out with Matthew and his friends. The Pharisees didn't like it. Jesus told them that doctors go to sick folks, and that God desires mercy, rather than mere ritualistic conformity to religious codes.

With other people Jesus was more gentle. Our minds might go to the woman caught in adultery, or the woman at the well (both women with complex marital situations, it seems). Jesus did not antagonise the needy, the broken, the hurting, the weak. When people were genuine, Jesus was more responsive. On this occasion a question came from the disciples of His cousin, John the Baptizer.

They had a simple question. He gave a simple answer. Why don't your disciples fast when all other Jewish disciples do? What makes your situation different? Jesus' answer? Me. That is, His disciples couldn't fast because He, the groom, was with them. When you are around the groom, mourning is not appropriate. He followed up with a critique of trying to squeeze His new way into the old wineskins of traditional religion. Something new and exciting was occurring, but let's not miss the point of the groom comment:

1. Jesus was explicit: I am the groom! He expected His hearers to ponder that truth and come to some sort of biblical conclusion about it. Perhaps He felt the Old Testament themes relating to divine marriage were so compelling that His hearers would hear Him right. Perhaps He wanted to intrigue folks and have them watch Him more closely.

2. Being with Jesus stirs great joy! If the Son of God has thrilled the heart of the Father for all eternity, and if being close to the groom is a reason for such great celebration,

then why do some followers of Jesus seem so negative about Him? We who know Jesus should, of all people, be the most joyful and celebratory. And yet …

3. Jesus anticipated that His followers would fast. When the groom is taken away, His followers should be so deeply bothered by His absence that the manifestation will be times of fasting and even mourning … not because of the state of the world, but because we so long for Him that we ache deep inside.

(See Matt. 9:14-17; Mark 2:18-22; and Luke 5:33-39.)

The Groom is Coming!

Jesus urged His followers to live in light of His identity as groom. He told them not to live anxiously as if they were in charge of their lives, but rather to live as if the God who made everything is taking care of them. The people of the world stress about stuff, but God's people have a greater caregiver than the world could ever afford. So they should live for God's kingdom, not for the kingdom of self or the kingdom of stuff. (And in Luke 12:32-34 He reveals a glimpse of our good God's heart by revealing that God intends to give them that kingdom!)

So how should such people live? They should live as if this world is not their home. They should live as if they are waiting for the return of their master. In Matthew 25:1-13 the focus is on being ready for the arrival of the bridegroom, so that those who are ready and waiting will get to go with him to the wedding feast. But when Jesus told a similar parable in Luke 12:35-40, there is an unexpected and thrilling twist. The slaves of the master are instructed to be dressed and ready to serve. Then, when the master returns, those slaves who are found up and waiting when the master returns will receive an amazing blessing. Do they get to go with him to the wedding? That might be what we would expect, but instead the reality is even better; the servants are told to recline at the table as the master gets dressed and ready to serve them!

We may accept the Bible speaking of Jesus as the groom, but many of us struggle to believe that we could really be the bride. This little story in Luke 12 drops to our level for a moment – we see we are merely slaves – but next thing you know, the master leaves the wedding and actually comes to serve us a feast! Maybe eternity won't be long enough to be fully convinced that God actually, really, truly loves us. Maybe in heaven we will watch the DVD of Jesus putting on the servant's garb and washing His disciples' feet, perhaps we should also ask to watch the less popular scene of Luke 12:35 and following. Or we could, of course, simply return to the cross and see self-giving love in its most vivid form. The greatest sacrifice of all time. For me.

15 Jesus the Marriage Advocate

• MATTHEW 19, JOHN 8, ETC

Many think of Christianity as a club for do-gooders, or a creed for conformists, or a hobby for the religious, or a fantasy for the gullible. It is easy to identify Christianity with a set of practices or beliefs or morals or institutions. But primarily it is one-ness with Jesus. Of course this works itself out in new practices, beliefs, behaviours and structures – all marriages bring such revolutions. But none of those externals lie at the heart of it. The heart of Christianity is Christ himself. And he is offered to you.[1]

GLEN SCRIVENER

---

1. Glen Scrivener, *321: The Story of God, the World, and You* (10Publishing, 2014), p. 106.

It was inevitable that Jesus' talk about weddings would bring questions about divorce. Actually, in those days, this was a hot topic of debate between different rabbis. Was it lawful to divorce for any reason at all, or just for marital unfaithfulness? There were different schools of thought. It would be tough to be married to the Rabbi that held the view that burnt toast was reason enough to hand over the divorce papers! (In a culture of increasingly easy, no-fault divorce, it still is tough to be married to a person with a low view of the permanence of marriage!)

When Jesus was asked if any-reason divorce was lawful, He did not respond with a contemporary analysis of societal norms. He did respond by describing God's original design. God created humans male and female. Male leaves his father and mother and becomes one flesh with his wife. Since they are now united by God, humans should not be separating. Simple. (Matt. 19:1-6)

The questioning Pharisees pushed back. Why did Moses tell folks to give a certificate of divorce and send the wife away? (See Deut. 24:1-4.) Jesus' response is incredibly enlightening. He does not explain the circumstances of Moses' instruction. Neither does He look to qualify Moses' authority. Very simply He puts His finger right on the issue. Moses did that because of their hardness of heart! Not their circumstances, nor their challenges, nor their difficulties, just because of their hearts. But again Jesus notes that the original plan was very different.

Jesus' follow up comment seems to tie Him to the other camp in the debate of that day. He states that there is one reason for divorce, and that is sexual immorality. Anything else, followed by remarriage to another, constitutes adultery. (Matt. 19:7-9)

Jesus set the marriage bar very high, and the disciples understood that. In fact, they responded by asking whether anyone can live up to His view of marriage. Perhaps it would be better to stay single? Jesus responded with a slightly cryptic saying.

Essentially Jesus said that singleness is hard. Then He gives three categories of eunuch. Some are such by birth, others by the acts of others, and still others by their own choice. This is getting uncomfortable – let's move on. Actually, pulling back from the spectre of castration, what is Jesus saying about marriage and singleness?

In Mark 10:1-12, we read the same story. It is followed, like Matthew 19, with the little children incident, and then the rich ruler and Jesus. So this is the same passage. But it has one difference. Mark does not include provision for divorce based on sexual immorality. The bar just got even higher.

Luke's Gospel also includes teaching from Jesus on this subject. Perhaps it was the same incident, or more likely, the same subject on a different occasion. Before Luke writes about divorce, we read that Jesus has just been teaching about the impossibility of loving God and money at the same time. A person will either love God or love themselves (using money as the mechanism to chase power, possessions, or whatever the goal is). If a person loves God and is faithful with what God entrusts to them, then they will be trusted with more (Luke 16:10-13).

Then Luke records the reaction of the Pharisees, who were lovers of money (and therefore not really lovers of God). They were ridiculing Jesus and He responded strongly against them, telling them that God sees past the show and knows their hearts. It feels like Luke is putting together several sayings of Jesus that would have been made in a conflict with the Pharisees – sort of a highlights reel. We don't read their questions or objections, just some of His best responses (Luke 16:14-15).

Jesus talks in verse 16 about the change since the coming of John the Baptist. Before John, the Old Covenant scriptures were the focus. Since John, the good news of the kingdom had been the focus. Maybe the law-sheriffs were feeling their power waning.

In verse 17 Jesus underscores the permanence of the revelation that is the Law – there is change, but there is not a dismissal of it. Presumably these men who were known for their concern for the Law, were either guilty of actually neglecting it (which we see stated elsewhere – Matthew 23:23), or they were accusing Jesus and His followers of breaking it (which we also see elsewhere, e.g. Matt. 12:1-2).

In verse 18, Jesus makes a statement about divorce and remarriage that appears to come out of the blue. Presumably, as we saw in Matthew and Mark, this would have been an issue they raised in their disputes with Jesus. Here's the statement:

> [18] 'Everyone who divorces his wife and marries another commits adultery, and he who marries a woman divorced from her husband commits adultery.'

Notice that Jesus is not resisting the existence of divorce. In a fallen world where people have hardened hearts, perhaps divorce is inevitable. This does not make it a positive thing – Malachi 2:16 (NASB) was clear, 'God hates divorce.' But again, His real point of resistance is against the idea of remarriage after divorce. Why? Presumably because Jesus knew His Old Testament, and He knew the role human marriage plays as the ultimate biblical image of the relationship between God and His people. Marriage is a key biblical motif that traces its way from cover to cover. Marriage is the uniting of male and female by the Spirit of God. In a fallen world, relationships will fail. But can something united by God be torn apart and separated, in order to free up the individuals to then be united with someone else? Not according to Jesus.

This will seem like a very hard position when viewed from our cultural perspective. But it is a position that we should all celebrate. Why? Because in light of the role of marriage in the story of the Bible, we do not want a God who has a casual view of divorce followed by remarriage. When it comes to struggling human marriages we tend to fall into two camps – either compassion for the individuals and a relaxed view of the institution of marriage, or a high view of marriage with a lack of compassion and understanding for those involved when it fails.

We should all celebrate that Jesus had such a high view of marriage. Being betrothed to someone with a low view creates great insecurity and hinders true unity. The Christ to whom we are betrothed has the highest view of marriage. We need not fear!

We should also appreciate just how compassionate Jesus was. If only the church could consistently offer passionate support for the biblical institution of marriage, combined with Christ-like compassion for every individual suffering in the complexities of marital struggles, betrayal, failure and difficulty.

The Compassionate Christ

We will be diving into John's Gospel in the next chapter, but let's sneak a peek at one incident. It sits between John 7 and 8, although scholars are not exactly sure where it belongs. The earliest and best manuscripts do not include this incident, so our Bibles will typically mark it off with a brief explanatory note to that effect.

This is not the place for a detailed explanation of how the manuscripts are evaluated to determine what should be included in our Bibles. However, at the risk of being too simplistic, there are two angles from which the experts come at this evaluation. On the one hand, they look at what they call 'external evidence' – this is about which manuscripts do and which do not include the text. On the other hand, they look at what they call 'internal evidence' – this involves evaluating the writing style, vocabulary, etc., of the content. Concerning this incident in John 7:53–8:11, the external evidence does not lead us to believe that it fits in its current place in the book of John. But the internal evidence supports the view that John wrote it. So it is included, and rightly so, but placed in the traditional location, which most scholars feel slightly awkward about (but have no better suggestions!)

So let's look at the story itself. Jesus was teaching at the temple when the scribes and Pharisees presented a woman to Him. She had been caught in the act of adultery and therefore, according to Leviticus 20:10, she should have been put to death. They were testing Him. This would be no test at all if Jesus was known for a hardline stance on everything addressed in the Law. But Jesus was an anomaly. He never sinned (although they thought He did), but He seemed to be willing to do things the Law forbade – apparently breaking the Sabbath, touching people with leprosy, etc. And certainly Jesus was known for showing compassion to individuals who were in a tough place. So they brought the woman to Him.

Would Jesus demonstrate a lack of compassion for the woman, thereby helping the crowds feel less drawn to this corrupt purveyor of grace? Or would Jesus condemn Himself as a lawbreaker by rejecting the Law of Moses? If they could trap Him into doing that, they would have a charge to then bring against Him.

So Jesus did the obvious thing. He bent down and starting writing in the dust. Maybe this is not so obvious, but it is intriguing. Dramatic videos make a big thing of this. Suddenly the dust cracks like great tablets of stone as the finger of God, in slow motion, inscribes some new legal code, and the Pharisees turn and run for cover! It is very dramatic. In actuality, after writing in the dust, Jesus then stood up and said something.

Jesus' words release Him from the Pharisees' trap, and extend hope to the woman. 'Let him who is without sin among you be the first to throw a stone at her.' One by one, each Pharisee turned and walked away. In the Sanhedrin, decisions would be voted on by the youngest first (to avoid undue influence from senior figures). Now John notes it is the older ones who walk away first. Perhaps their greater years made their personal catalogue of private sin more extensive. Soon the woman was left alone before Jesus.

He asked where her accusers were and who was left to condemn her. No one. So the story ends with Jesus' words. 'Neither do I condemn you,' – compassion. 'Go, and from now on sin no more' – high view of marital fidelity and purity.

What had He written in the dust? Was it a list of their sins? Was it a list of their mistresses? People love to speculate. We don't know. What we do know is that Jesus was able to maintain a very high view of marriage, while showing wonderful compassion to those caught on the rough edges of life. Maybe we should ponder how we can do the same today – not one or the other, but both.

16 Jesus the Bridegroom

• JOHN 1–4

'That joining together of Head and members, that indwelling of Christ in our hearts – in short, that mystical union – are accorded by us the highest degree of importance, so that Christ, having been made ours, makes us sharers with him in the gifts with which he has been endowed. We do not, therefore, contemplate him outside ourselves from afar in order that his righteousness may be imputed to us but because we put on Christ and are engrafted into his body – in short, because he deigns to make us one with him.' [1]

JOHN CALVIN

1. John Calvin, *Institutes,* 3.11.10.

Why are we so dejected as if we had not such a rich husband? All our husband's riches are ours for our good, we receive of it in our measure, why do we not go to the fountain and make use of it? Why, in the midst of abundance, are we poor and beggarly? Here we may see the misery of the world.

Men live as if Christ were nothing, or did nothing concern them, as if he were a person abstracted from them, as if he were not a head or husband, as if he had received the Spirit only for himself and not for them, whereas all that is in Christ is for us. I beseech you therefore let us learn to know Christ better.[2]

RICHARD SIBBES

The Gospel of John has three introductions. There is the famous prologue in 1:1-18 which introduces Him as the Word. The rest of the first chapter is also introductory, with multiple testimonies identifying Jesus as the central character in the book. Furthermore, chapters 2–4 are an extended introduction laying out key themes and ideas that will swirl their way through the tensions that follow.

Three introductions: the prologue, the first chapter, the first four chapters. And the relational themes of marriage and union run through all three. Once you turn to the fifth chapter, the tensions really ramp up as Jesus heals a lame man on a Sabbath. From that point on Jesus is a marked man and the intrigue of His conflict with the Jews moves to centre stage.

---

2. Richard Sibbes, 'A Description of Christ,' *The Complete Works of Richard Sibbes*, vol. 1 (Edinburgh: The Banner of Truth Trust, 1973), p. 21.

The Prologue (1:1-18)

Using the opening phrase from Genesis 1:1, John looks back to the very beginning and makes overt in one verse what we took a whole chapter to explore at the start of this book. In the beginning God … was in fellowship. The Word was with God. Out of that communion creation and all of history were born, but it started with Trinitarian communion. God's closeness to God. A God in fellowship with one called 'the Word' – this hints at a God who speaks, who talks, who listens, who communicates and who communes.

Most mythical gods dwell in great and terrible darkness. But God's Word had life in Himself and was, Himself, the light of men. We are in darkness, but He shines as light.

In fact, God repeatedly takes the initiative to reach out to humanity. He sent a man called John to bear witness about the light. Then the true light Himself came into the world. We didn't know Him. In fact, even His own people did not receive Him. But here is the glorious gospel breaking in: to all who did receive Him, that is, those who trusted in His name, they are given the right to become children of God – not on a human level or by human initiative, but by God's desire and will.

So the One who used to meet with Moses in the tent down by the camp, the One whose repeated face to face company gave Moses the confidence to ask to see the glory of the LORD who was up on the mountain, that One became flesh and pitched His tent among us again. Verses 14-18 are bubbling over with seven or eight references and allusions to Exodus 33–34. As the Word became flesh we have seen His glory and His glory is full of grace and truth. (Read with your Old Testament lenses on: He was full of *steadfast love* and *faithfulness*, the often repeated Old Testament adjectives used to describe God.) The law came through Moses but this grace and truth came through Jesus Christ. Indeed, nobody has seen God, including Moses on the mountain. God's face was not to be seen. But the only God, Jesus Christ, who is at the Father's side, who pitches His tent down near the people, He has made God known!

This Word, Jesus Christ, was forever relationally close to the Father (1;1, 2). This God, Jesus Christ, is at the Father's side, near to the heart of the Father (1:18). Later, in John 13, we glimpse this same picture as John leans against Jesus as the disciples recline together during a meal. This is an image of intimacy and close fellowship. That same Christ has come toward us, to bring to us the same kind of relational intimacy with God.

The Introduction of Testimonies (1:19-51)

The introduction to Jesus and the gospel continues through the rest of chapter 1. It reads like an anthology of testimonies. As characters are introduced to Jesus walking in their midst, we as readers are introduced to Him too.

John the Baptist – John was a great man of great humility. He pointed to Christ and was happy with no praise or recognition. He wasn't Elijah, or the promised prophet. He was simply the voice of Isaiah 40, the voice that prepared the way for the Lord Himself. He was a baptizer, but only with water. Compared to the prophet he spoke of, John was not even in the same category – a servant may not be in the league of the VIP guest of honour, but at least the servant gets to untie the VIP's sandal. But John was not worthy even to do that. John was a great man, but he knew that Jesus was infinitely greater.

When he saw Jesus coming toward him he declared Him to be the Lamb of God who takes away the sin of the world. John had been told by God that he would see the Spirit descend and remain on the Anointed One who would anoint others with the Spirit. Thus when he saw the Spirit descend upon Jesus, he bore witness that this was indeed the Son of God. The anointing of Jesus with the Spirit is a subtle precursor to Jesus' role of anointing others with the Spirit. The Spirit who will unite a redeemed humanity with God's Son!

Andrew, Peter's brother – Andrew had been a disciple of John, until he was pointed to Jesus. Very simply, he testified to Peter that they had found the Messiah, and then brought him to Jesus.

Philip and Nathanael – Philip was called by Jesus and then immediately found Nathanael and told him about Jesus. Here we read that Jesus was the fulfilment of both the books of Moses and the Prophets. The testimonies are piling up! But the punch line goes to sceptical Nathanael.

Just before Nathanael meets Jesus, he is questioning whether anything good can come out of Nazareth. (Technically this was a fair question, for Nazareth was not a place with a great reputation.) Next thing we know he is giving the punch line to the chapter – 'You are the Son of God! You are the King of Israel!' What we know is that Jesus started off their conversation by identifying Nathanael as a true Israelite, one without any deceit in him. Nathanael was confused, how could Jesus know him? So Jesus told him that He had seen him under the fig tree earlier. Suddenly Nathanael blurts his testimony. Is that not an over-reaction, even though Jesus' awareness was miraculously impressive? Let's speculate about what was going on.

Could it be that Nathanael was reading the story of Jacob when he was under the fig tree? Jacob was Mr Israel, Mr

Deceiver himself. In contrast, Jesus recognises something in Nathanael (a man in whom there is no deceit) that contrasts with Jacob. Who knows, perhaps Nathanael had even been praying about his own character in light of Jacob's. If this was the case, it would mean that Jesus not only was aware of the location of Nathanael, but also his thoughts and prayers. Nathanael blurts out his testimony, 'Rabbi, you are the Son of God! You are the King of Israel!' And just to make sure we get it, John then reports Jesus' follow up comment … a reference to Jacob's vision at Bethel of the stairway connecting humanity and God's throne. Only now it is not a stairway forming the connection – it is the Son of Man Himself! Nathanael got to make the punch line, but perhaps Jesus' own testimony is really the main point!

The Extended Introduction: Cana to Cana, Jews and Non-Jews (John 2-4)

The introduction to John's gospel continues in extended form through chapters two, three and four. This section begins with a miraculous sign in Cana and ends with another one. In between there is a double sequence of stories. First we see a Jewish group, followed by a non-Jewish group, both gradually grasping who Jesus is. In each chapter there is confusion over literal versus spiritual interpretation of Jesus' words, as well as a wedding reference or hint.

The Wedding at Cana – The action begins at a wedding where Jesus first manifests His glory. Perhaps this is the perfect start to the selected signs sequence in John's gospel. Why? Because the glory revealed is not primarily His power, but His abundance, His generosity, even His sensitivity at a wedding.

176

When the wedding wine ran out, Jesus saved the host from great shame, and in fact gave the generous gift of a better wine as the party continued. This was the first sign by which He revealed something of His glory – and maybe the sign was intended to reveal the kind of God He represented, the kind of God who would take a wedding on the rocks and turn it into a party to remember. Generous, abundant, prodigious. Jesus performed a sign and people started to believe in Him.

Is a miracle-based belief in Jesus enough? For many churches today, any belief will do. Converts and adherents add numbers, so any convert counts. But throughout John's gospel we are led to wrestle with the notion of inadequate belief. For Jesus, inadequate belief is just that: inadequate. The rest of chapter 2 makes that clear. Jesus never seems to be concerned with building a following. His concern is for a spiritual union with people – deeper, closer, more connected.

Temple Cleansing – As Jesus arrived in Jerusalem, He launched His ministry with a high-impact entrance. He made a whip and drove out of the temple courts all the sellers and money-changers. That would have created a stir. The other Gospels report that He did this again in His Passion Week visit to the temple. Perhaps once was troubling, but twice was unacceptable to the religious elite who ran the bazaar?

Naturally the local leadership wanted to know where He received the authority to commit such a bold act. They asked for a sign. Jesus offered them the seventh of the seven signs in John's Gospel – His own resurrection. (You didn't miss the other five between the wedding at Cana and here … the rest are still to come, but this is the seventh that is anticipated from almost the beginning of the sequence.)

The end of the chapter offers a slightly cryptic transition. Apparently many trusted in Jesus because of His signs, but He did not entrust Himself to them. Why? Because, John tells us, Jesus knew what was in man. Then he demonstrates that to us, because in the next sentence he introduces an example man: 'Now there was a man…'

Nicodemus – Nicodemus turns out to be John's example of a man who was impressed by Jesus' signs, but didn't really believe in Jesus. He came to Jesus late one night for a quiet chat. Perhaps he could sense trouble brewing. Last time a prophet from God had burst on the scene the religious leadership had not handled it too well and it turned into a PR disaster. This time Nic takes the initiative. He was the minister of education, the teacher of Israel. He came to Jesus, perhaps, as my friend likes to suggest, to confer on Him an honorary doctorate and thereby get Him under control for the Jerusalem elite.

So Nicodemus launches into his buttering-up speech – 'Rabbi, we know that you are a teacher come from God, for no one can do these signs that you do unless God is with him.' Nice start. So did Jesus respond with a polite head nod and reciprocate with a 'pleasure to meet you' kind of response? Not at all. Jesus goes right to the heart of the matter. Essentially Jesus says this, 'I can't talk to you about spiritual things because you haven't been born into a new life by the Spirit – you don't have the Spirit.'

Oh dear. This doesn't feel like the right response from Jesus. Unless, of course, He knew what He was doing. Jesus wasn't going to get into a religious discussion with Nicodemus, no matter how much learning he had, without first pointing out that he did not have the prerequisite ingredient for true connection with God – the Spirit. In the course of the next verses Jesus touched on ideas from Ezekiel 36 (born of water and the Spirit), Deuteronomy 30 (he who ascended and descended), and Numbers 21 (Moses lifted up the serpent in the wilderness). But maybe the biggest Old Testament allusion of all is to Genesis 3. Nicodemus you are not alive; you need to be born from above; you need to have the Spirit of life restored before we can chitchat about the kingdom of God. Nicodemus, like everyone else, was taken off guard. Why do I need to be born? I'm already alive!

So we come to the glorious ground-zero gospel passage of the Bible. Just like in Moses' day when the brass serpent was elevated on a pole, so Jesus would be lifted up on a cross. In order to have life we must look to Him. Look, and live. Simple. That is the gospel of salvation by grace through faith and not by works. God loved, God gave, so just believe and receive.

The Nicodemus story doesn't reference marital themes directly. But the focus on the Spirit is significant. At the core of the Gospel message is the role of the Holy Spirit. This is true in the born-into-the-family theme here, in the adopted-into-the-family theme in Paul's later writings, and it is true in the married-into-the-family theme that we are tracing. In fact, that marital theme soon shows up in John's gospel:

John the Baptist – Halfway through chapter 3 there is a scene change. Some of John the Baptist's disciples got into a discussion with a Jew about purification rituals. This prompted them to come to John and ask about Jesus. Specifically, they pointed out that the crowds were now thronging to Jesus instead of to John. The overwhelming flood of people flocking to John had dwindled to a mere trickle. They had a point. John the Baptist had been the big news in Judea until Jesus showed up. Now it looked like his Baptism ministry was drying up!

John's response is to talk about weddings (see 3:27-30). He had told them from the start that his ministry was one of preparation for the coming Christ (see Malachi 3:1). So, John explained, the bride is with the bridegroom, which is only right. The best man, or friend of the bridegroom, is excited at the coming of the bridegroom, because the wedding is about his friend the groom, not himself. Rather than resenting the change in ministry fortunes, John was completely joyful about the crowd heading to Jesus, because the bride should always go to the groom! Indeed, John could say, 'He must increase but I must decrease.'

In these three stories, we see a progression of levels of belief among the Jews. The folks at the temple didn't get who Jesus was, or what was going on (even though they seemed to believe in Him). Nicodemus fared marginally better. John the Baptist really grasped it all. Now let's watch a progression among Gentiles:

A Woman at a Well – Jesus needed to head back up to Galilee, not least to get back to Cana for the second sign that would tie this first section of the Gospel together! Due to racial tensions, Jews would typically take a detour across the Jordan in order to avoid Samaria. This time Jesus took the direct route and came to Sychar. It was lunchtime. Jesus was tired and He sat down by the well as His disciples headed up the path into the town to get some food.

With the safe assumption that Jesus knew His Old Testament, He probably knew what would come next. Sitting by a foreign well in Bible times seems to have been the best way to go 'dear hunting' (don't forget chapter 4 of this book!). Sure enough, a woman approached.

This was an awkward situation. Jewish and Samaritan. Male and female. Alone. Jesus asked for a drink and she answered by highlighting the racial awkwardness. Samaritans and Jews didn't mix.

Jesus by-passed the awkwardness and pressed on with His request. He pointed out that if she knew who He was, *she* would have asked *Him* for water, because He could give living water. Living water means moving water – as in a stream, or plumbed into a house, without anything green growing on it. Living water was a luxury in those days. He didn't mean luxury water, though, He meant something even better. She took Him to be referring to something physical, but He meant something spiritual.

Nicodemus and this woman were opposites. One came by night, the other by day. One wanted to see Jesus; one didn't plan to chat. One was male; the other was female. One was highly esteemed and powerful; the other was probably despised by every woman in town. One was at the top of any social totem pole; the other avoided anything social. But this they had in common: when Jesus meant spiritual, they both took it as literal.

So what was Jesus referring to? A spring of water welling up within? This is Old Testament language for the Holy Spirit and the New Covenant promises. So she replied with a 'yes please'. Actually, it is hard to tell her tone. She probably thought Jesus was trying to flirt with her. As it turns out, that was her life's pattern, so maybe she saw all this living water talk as some sort of verbal trap leading to her agreeing to give Jesus her phone number (not literally, metaphorically). 'Okay, go ahead, give me the water …'

Jesus revealed that He wasn't there for good old biblical well-side dating. He told her to go and call her husband. When she revealed she didn't have one, Jesus followed through with some insight a stranger should not have had. He told her that He knew she didn't have a husband, although she'd had five, and now she was living with a man who wasn't her husband! This insight dramatically caught her attention. Suddenly Jesus went from being a Jew, to a sir, and now to a prophet.

Jesus is sitting at a well, talking to a woman about issues of marriage. Surely this is no coincidence? Would the Messiah Himself seek a bride from among non-Jewish people? John 4 opens up that possibility. She changed the subject from her private life to religion, which Jesus was more than happy to talk about. But let's not skim past her private life so fast. Five husbands!? We can only speculate as to whether this was five divorces, or widowed five times, which would be unfortunate (and either way, it might raise some questions about her cooking!).

As their conversation continued, Jesus spoke of God seeking true worshippers. Again, the real issue was not something physical (like the location of a temple), but the inner spiritual reality that He had come to inaugurate in the New Covenant. The woman believed in the Samaritan idea of a coming Messiah, so she told Him that. Jesus replied, 'I am.' Wide open admission. No hiding. What incredible grace He showed to Ms Nobody. This woman, the lowest of the low, and probably despised by every woman in her town, now gets a plain introduction to the Messiah Himself!

At that point the disciples returned and awkwardly stared at Jesus who was talking with this woman. They couldn't ask her what she wanted as it would implicate Him. They couldn't ask Him either. So they gawped. She grew understandably uncomfortable and rushed off to give her testimony to the folks in the town.

Jesus then engaged His disciples in conversation about food. But not about literal food. It was their turn to miss His point. And they did miss it, with style. They urged Him to eat but He told them He had food to eat that they didn't know about. While they were wondering who slipped Jesus a kebab, He invited them into a work more satisfying than any meal – that of harvesting souls. They didn't get it. So He told them to lift up their eyes and look. What they saw was a town full of people, hoisting their skirts and running across the field. A wave of white coming to Jesus. Like a harvest. Or even, like a bride.

If John the Baptist could have heard about this scene, he would have loved it!

So chapters two to three show a progression of belief among Jews, with an emphasis on the work of the Spirit and marital imagery at the conclusion. Chapter four gives progressing belief among these Gentile townsfolk, with early reference to the Holy Spirit and marital imagery throughout.

Finally, the opening section of John comes to a close with the second sign, back in Cana. Jesus heals an official's son. This sign involves a two-part belief from the father. He believed when Jesus spoke the word, and then his belief was driven deeper when he realised that miles away, at that very moment his son was healed. Surely belief is being set up to be a key theme throughout John's Gospel. But what about marital themes? Will they appear again?

17 Jesus the Builder

• JOHN 14–16

The central reality of the Christian life is that believers are united to Christ, and the reason this is so central is because it links us to the central relationship that there is, Christ's relationship to his Father. … The early church recognized this, and so they wrote of salvation by writing of the God in whom we participate when we are saved.[1]

Donald Fairbairn

Jesus prays that they may *be brought to complete unity,* sharing richly in both the unity of purpose and the wealth

---

1. Donald Fairbairn, *Life in the Trinity: An Introduction to Theology with the Help of the Church Fathers* (Downers Grove, IL: IVP, 2009), p. 202.

of love that tie the Father and the Son together. The purpose, as in v. 21, is *to let the world know that you sent me,* to which is now added the further goal, *that you … have loved them even as you have loved me.* The thought is breathtakingly extravagant.[2]

D. A. CARSON

The next section of John's Gospel, chapters 5–12, is rich in many themes, and we will come back to some highlights in the next chapter of this book. But for a strong development of the marital theme, let's jump forward to the other end of Jesus' ministry: the Upper Room.

Starting in chapter 13, this section of the Gospel is thick with tension. Jesus was leaving and the disciples couldn't easily come to terms with that. Jesus' handling of His disciples is so tender and encouraging. It all starts with Jesus taking the menial servant's role and washing the disciples' feet. The room was thick with an ethos of love, as demonstrated by Jesus. For Judas, the room probably felt starved of oxygen. When a person is not responsive to Christ, then acts of love are repulsive and tend to choke out the imposter.

Jesus then revealed to Judas that He knew of his plan to betray Him. So Judas had to spring into action. The plot to arrest Jesus had been brewing since chapter 5, but this Passover was the festival when it had to happen. Jesus' dramatic raising of Lazarus had seen to that. So the Jews planned to get Him after the festival, before He could hit the road for Galilee. Judas was going to help. Why? In chapter 12 Judas had seen a massive potential donation to the ministry fund broken and poured out on to Jesus. This extravagant

2. D. A. Carson, *The Gospel According to John*, Pillar New Testament Commentary (Grand Rapids: Eerdmans, 1991), p. 569.

devotion from Mary meant no cash to plunder for Judas. This infuriated Judas, so he had agreed to betray Jesus.

As Judas slunk into the night, Jesus launched a volley of great Gospel of John themes. 'Now is the Son of Man glorified!' (His 'hour' had always been future until this point.) The glory references continue, followed by a new commandment – to love one another. This would become the defining feature of being a follower of Christ. This great commandment is not just a pragmatic suggestion to aid mission efficacy. This is to be the distinguishing characteristic of Jesus followers, because this is the distinguishing characteristic of Jesus Himself!

So as we come to the end of chapter 13, Peter is boldly declaring that he will follow Jesus even to death. Jesus informs him that his zeal to follow won't even last the night.

Comfort in Wedding Terms

The disciples were disturbed. Jesus was leaving and He told them they could not go with Him. So at the start of chapter 14, Jesus begins His comforting speech by offering a compelling marital image.

Jesus spoke of His Father's house and its many rooms. The Jewish disciples would not have taken long to get what He was referring to here. It was standard practice for a would-be husband to go home alone and prepare a housing extension for his new wife to come and join him. Jesus spoke of His Father's house having many rooms. This was a lavish and extravagant house.

Jesus said He was going to prepare a place in His Father's house. Specifically, He was going to prepare a place, 'for you.' The marital theme here should overwhelm any speculation about the nature of the room/place/mansion. A bride-to-be is much more comforted by the fact that her groom is preparing a place for them to be together, than she is by how nice the place itself will be. Sadly, too many Christians are more focused on the building materials in heaven than the builder. The disciples were pondering Christ's departure with sadness, but this talk of preparing a place launched a speech of great comfort for them.

Jesus assured them of His return to collect His bride. The fact that He was thinking about the accommodations in His Father's home, and that He was going to do some building there, meant that He was planning to come back again. The groom would build the extension for his new bride and then come to get her. The goal was never a building project; it was a marriage. The goal was to be together.

I know that men reading this may struggle with the idea of Jesus as their groom. I don't think the disciples did. They had been with Jesus for three years. This band of brothers had grown very close and they were deeply troubled by their leader's departure. His use of marital language to offer assurance of their being together again worked for them because it was the strongest relational language possible. But there was more ...

The Union Comforter

In the second half of chapter 14, Jesus introduced another source of comfort. Yes, His departure could be less traumatic when they knew why He was leaving: to prepare a place to be together again, forever. But more than that, Jesus planned to ask His Father to give them another helper, another comforter.

There are two ways to say 'another' ... and in this case Jesus means another of the same kind as Himself. Just as

He had been a helper and comforter for them, so this other helper would be the same. Jesus was going to ask His Father to send them the Spirit of truth.

Along with references to the Holy Spirit, there is another reference that should catch our attention as we trace the marital theme through Scripture. Take verse 20 for example, 'In that day you will know that I am in my Father, and you in me, and I in you.' Jesus is speaking about coming to the disciples in the person of the Spirit. Then they will know that Jesus is in the Father, and there is a mutual indwelling between disciples and Jesus; Jesus and disciples. What does this mean?

John's Gospel is full of references from Jesus about His relationship with His Father. In just over 400 sentences of Jesus talking in John's Gospel (think red-letter text in a red-letter Bible), there are almost 200 references to the Father-Son connection. Some of these references are straightforward: the Father sent the Son, the Father gave the Son authority, etc. But quite a number are speaking of Father and Son mutually indwelling each other. This is that relationship we saw back in chapter one of this book.

Now, in this section, Jesus starts to speak of the disciples and Jesus mutually indwelling each other, just as the Father and the Son do. In this sense human marriage is a picture of the Trinity. The Father and the Son are one, united in the love communicated by the Spirit. So a husband and wife are one, united in shared love communicated by the Spirit – true Christian marriage is Trinitarian because of the role of the Spirit in the relationship. So Jesus is describing His relationship with His disciples in essentially marital terms – I in you and you in me.

Preparing a place is one thing – but being united by the Spirit in a relationship like the Father and Son share, that is taking it to a whole new level! This passage is comfort indeed for those disciples facing up to the soon departure of their Lord.

Jesus went on to talk about the Father and Son 'making our home' with the believer who loves Jesus and keeps His word. The giving of the Spirit would give peace to these troubled men. Instead of their being troubled, Jesus wanted them to lean into the new relational arrangement that would soon exist.

Oneness Described by Metaphor

Jesus shifted from the marital image to another relational one. 'I am the vine; you are the branches. Whoever abides in me and I in him, he it is that bears much fruit, for apart from me you can do nothing.' (15:5) The vine and its branches are a picture of absolute dependence and relational interconnectedness. The branches bear fruit, but only because they remain in the vine.

In verse 9, Jesus makes a stunning statement. 'As the Father has loved me, so have I loved you. Abide in my love.' When the text says 'as' we need to pause and take it in. The Father loved the Son. How? Perfectly, fully, for all eternity, without any hesitation or limitation. In the same way, the Son loved His disciples. Now He was inviting them to linger in that love.

As the passage progresses, the 'as' and 'just as' statements should grab our attention. The connection between the believer and Jesus will again be compared to the perfect relationship between the Father and the Son. The greater our gaze on the Trinity, the more our hearts will be blown open by this upper room discourse!

Of course, throughout this section Jesus is instructing His disciples on the importance of their love for each other. That was the new commandment back in chapter 13. We must ponder that commandment and be sure to let it mark our lives and churches. But let's not make the mistake of focusing on that and losing sight of the wonderful love that births such love in us. John would later write that we love because He first loved us (1 John 4:19). We can never look too long into the love of God for God, or the love of God for humanity.

Shared Experience

In the second half of chapter 15, Jesus connects His disciples to Himself with the language of servant and master. Since the world has hated and persecuted Jesus, so it will hate and persecute His servants. The coming of the Spirit will prove significant though, because the Spirit will bear witness about the Son to the disciples, and they, in turn, will bear witness about the Son. Whether the metaphor is marriage, vine, or master-servant, it is the Spirit that unites the Son and His disciples, resulting in a deeply shared experience.

All that belongs to the Father also belongs to the Son. And it is the Spirit who will bring all of those blessings to the bride of the Son. So as chapter 16 moves towards its conclusion, the emphasis on the Spirit continues as Jesus speaks of the role of the Spirit to give, to communicate, and to point to Christ.

Jesus both comforted and prepared His disciples for their coming experience of separation from Him and persecution from the world. Jesus wanted them to be ready for life without Him alongside them. Actually, not having Him with them meant that they could, by the Spirit, have the greater privilege of Jesus inside them. Jesus was going back to His Father, but this meant that the coming Spirit would bring the life of God, Father and Son, into the hearts of the followers.

Please don't miss 16:26-27. Jesus wanted His followers to grasp that in Him they had full access to the Father. So He told them that He wouldn't be asking the Father on their behalf. Being in the family means being in the family! The Father *Himself* loved them. Again, how easy for us to walk past this truth and miss it. Just a chapter later we see Jesus praying for downstream disciples like us, and stating that the Father loves us even as He loved the Son. (See 17:23 and be sure to highlight it!) But so many of us don't believe that. We've been trained by a simple-legal gospel to think that the Father is angry and the Son is our kind lawyer ready to defend us. However, put the simple-legal gospel into full marital terms and we are one with the Son, and therefore fully loved by His Father! I have seen people stumble over, and then have their hearts ignited by John 16:27 and 17:23. But why does the Father's love for us surprise us? After all, what does John 3:16 say? Oh yes, it is the Father that loved the world and gave His Son. Strangely we seem to miss even that verse!

The Holy of Holies

Surely John 17 is like the holiest Bible ground for us? To listen in to Jesus praying to His Father like this is truly remarkable. We looked at this prayer in chapter 1, so we won't go over it in detail, but let's enjoy a few highlights.

With the theme of marriage swirling in our thinking, let's look at the relationship of the Trinity that we find in this prayer. Jesus wanted the Father to glorify Him so that He could glorify the Father in return. He planned to give eternal life to the people the Father had given Him, and He defined eternal life – it is to know the only true God and Jesus Christ, who was sent by the Father.

The love relationship of the Trinity is truly glorious to consider. Try to imagine the Father's eternal delight in the Son, and the Son's eternal response of love to the Father. That loving interaction by the Spirit is so pure and wonderful that it radiates, it is glorious! And then try to ponder that we are invited into that!

Jesus prayed for His disciples (vv. 9-19). He prayed for them to be kept by the Father, guarded and protected in a dangerous and antagonistic world. He prayed for them to be set apart by the Word of God and the Spirit of God. Then He prayed for those who would believe in Him based on their words – i.e. us! (see vv. 20-26)

Jesus' prayer for us, His disciples, was that we would be one. He prays this twice; His goal is that the world will know and believe that the Father sent Him. This oneness is not a polite shared cup of tea kind of oneness. It is 'just as' the Father is in the Son, and the Son in the Father; in the same way, it is us in them! This kind of us in them unity is profoundly marital, even without any overt marital terms being used here. To be one like the Father and the Son are one, by mutual indwelling through the Spirit, this is what marital oneness is supposed to represent!

Jesus wants us to be with Him (in the place He is preparing for us). Why? So that we can see Jesus' glory, given by the Father before the foundation of the world. And don't miss the motivation. The Father glorifies the Son for one reason – because He loves Him. Again, this is a picture of marriage, and true marriage is a picture of this heavenly relationship. One spouse will always praise the other because of love. The gritted teeth, so called, 'act of the will' kind of glory giving that we often see encouraged by the church is really a bizarre religious phenomenon. Everywhere else people know that glory is given because of devotion. It is true in sports, in marketing, in relationships, everywhere. People give glory because of devotion to the other. This is true in the Trinity. The only place people seem to celebrate glorifying another without true motivation is in the church. Perhaps it shouldn't exist there either.

We can clearly see that the theme of marriage is very present in John's Gospel. But if we scratch the surface, there is a much richer vein of marital imagery. The language of 'I in you and you in me' speaks of a mutual indwelling that is Trinitarian, and by extension, marital. The role of the Spirit in uniting believers to Christ, again, is marital. The relational language of abiding in this section of John, as well as the wedding language, reinforces the truth that God desires a deep marital bond with His people.

Before we move on to the rest of the New Testament, let's look at the final section of the Gospel – what we might term 'the marriage proposal'.

18 Jesus' Great Union Proposal

• JOHN 18–20

Christ is the first object of faith, before any benefit or gift that we have from him; first, we must receive Christ before we have any grace, or favour, or strength, from him. And a sanctified soul looks first to Christ, to the love of Christ, to the person of Christ, and then to his goods and his riches. As one that is married, she regards first the person of her husband, and then looks to the enjoyment of his goods, and inheritance, and nobilities, or else it is no better than a harlot's love.[1]

RICHARD SIBBES

---

1. Richard Sibbes, 'The Fountain Opened,' *The Complete Works of Richard Sibbes*, Vol. 5 (Edinburgh: The Banner of Truth Trust, 1973), p. 516.

Behold, he has put his people into the hands of his dear Son. He has even put us into Christ's body; 'for we are members of his body, of his flesh, and of his bones.' He sees us in Christ to have died, in him to have been buried, and in him to have risen again. As the Lord Jesus Christ is well-pleasing to the Father, so in him are we well-pleasing to the Father also; for our being in him identifies us with him ... . Firmly believe that until the Lord rejects Christ he cannot reject his people; until he repudiates the atonement and the resurrection, he cannot cast away any of those with whom he has entered into covenant in the Lord Jesus Christ.[2]

CHARLES HADDON SPURGEON

What is John's big goal as he describes the death and resurrection of Jesus? It could be argued that his goal is for all people to be drawn to Christ, just as he had said would happen. Three times John records Jesus predicting that He will be 'lifted up.' Let's consider those passages before we focus on the event of His death itself.

John 3:14 – We have already looked at John 3 and Jesus' conversation with Nicodemus. This scholar and senior figure in the Jewish Sanhedrin couldn't really engage with what Jesus was saying. This was not because Nicodemus did not know the Hebrew Scriptures – he certainly did. He couldn't understand Jesus' teaching because he didn't have new life from the Spirit of God. As Jesus spoke to him He reminded him of the incident in Numbers 21. The people of Israel complained against God and so He

2. Charles Haddon Spurgeon, 'Perseverence in Holiness,' in *Metropolitan Tabernacle Pulpit*, Vol. 35 (Pasadena, TX: Pilgrim, 1975), p. 547, cited in Johnson, p. 176.

sent vipers among them. People were being bitten and were dying. Moses came to God and was told to make a bronze serpent on a pole.

Since Genesis 3 is very much in the background to the conversation between Jesus and Nicodemus, it would make sense for that bronze serpent to have its head skewered on the wooden stake, and then for its body to be wrapped around the pole in its death throes. This was a dead serpent, a judged serpent – sin dealt with as promised in Genesis 3:15. So the people were told that when they were bitten, they needed to do nothing, but just to look and live.

In the same way, 'the Son of Man must be lifted up, so that whoever believes in him may have eternal life.' Look and live. Jesus was going to be lifted up like that bronze serpent, and this time sin would be dealt with and judged, in Jesus! The only right response of a human would be to look and live.

John 8:28 – From John chapter 5 onwards there is an informal trial of Jesus occurring. The religious leaders in Jerusalem took exception to Jesus working on the Sabbath and then making Himself equal with His Father. Over the next chapters, and months, they sought to trap Him in His words and get an accusation to stick. In chapter 8 it had been six months since the initial incident, but Jesus' provocative healing of the lame man in chapter 5 is still lingering in the background.

By chapter 8 it is autumn and Jesus is at the Feast of Booths in Jerusalem. Jesus was stirring up tension among the religious leadership with His words to them. In verse 21 He launches into a speech with references to leaving them to die in their sin. They got confused about where He was going and who He was. Jesus said, 'I told you that you would die in your sins, for unless you believe that I am, you will die in your sins.' (This literal translation reveals one of the so-called 'I am' statements that John has woven into his gospel. There are seven famous 'I am' statements that are completed with a description: I am the good shepherd, I am the light of the world, etc. But this is one of another set of 'I am' statements, ones which do not have a description following. The most famous of them comes at the end of chapter 8, in verse 58 where Jesus says, 'Before Abraham was, I am'.)

So, in verse 28, Jesus gives another 'I am' as He gives them an explanation as to when they would discover His identity. 'When you have lifted up the Son of Man, then you will know that I am ...' Their crucifying of Jesus would make clear to them that He was who He claimed to be.

John 12:32 – The final 'lifted up' reference comes in the hinge section of the book, chapter 12. Jesus is arriving in Jerusalem when some Greek visitors ask Philip if they can see Jesus. (Philip was the only disciple with a Greek name, so it makes sense that they approached him.) Philip grabbed Andrew and together they came to ask Jesus about the Greeks. We looked at this conversation back in chapter 1 of this book, but let's review the highlights. Bizarrely, Jesus then launched into a speech about His being glorified and some insight into farming and seeds needing to die to bear fruit.

Perhaps you can imagine the confused shrug of Andrew and Philip, followed by a, *'Yes, of course, but about the Greeks ...'* But Jesus continued with some talk about people who would serve Him and what that would look like. *'Serve you, right, but about the Greeks?'*

Jesus pressed on to describe how He was troubled, but He wanted the Father to glorify His own name. At that moment a voice thundered from heaven, 'I have glorified it, and will glorify it again!' Everyone was rightly amazed by this supernatural sound. Perhaps Andrew and Philip exclaimed along with the others, 'Wow! Was that God's voice, or was that thunder?' But then back to the matter in hand, *Jesus, about the Greeks …'*

Jesus carried on by explaining that judgment time had come and the ruler of the world would be cast out. *'The Greeks…?'* And then He answered their question in verse 32, 'And I, when I am lifted up from the earth, will draw all people to myself.' There is the answer. Jesus is about to die, which is His glorification, and through His death He will draw all nations, all people, to Himself.

Just in case we think He might be talking about His ascension, John makes it clear that the 'lifted up' phrase is pointing to the manner of His death. Jesus died to draw people from every nation to Himself. Here is the groom preparing to propose to the bride.

The Passion – The first scene in John's passion narrative is the arrest in the Garden of Gethsemane. This concludes with Jesus stopping Simon Peter's awkward rescue attempt and stating, 'Shall I not drink the cup that the Father has given me?' This statement forms an *inclusio* (book end) with the 'I am thirsty' statement and the drink that Jesus will take on the cross.

After His arrest, Jesus was taken first to Annas – the power broker behind the scenes in Jerusalem. Annas had been high priest and now effectively controlled the position that his son-in-law, Caiaphas, currently occupied. Annas ran the marketplace in the temple and was used to pulling all the strings. But he got nowhere with Jesus! Annas' failed attempts to get Jesus to say something incriminating about His teaching or His followers was an early hint of the desperation of the leadership. Annas' power amounted to nothing as he discovered that Jesus was really the one in charge during this interrogation – Jesus' calm and dignified authority must have ruffled Annas greatly.

John tells us nothing of the two trials before Caiaphas and the Sanhedrin. He doesn't mention the night trial or the early morning trial. Instead, the next event John records is Jesus being taken to Pontius Pilate.

John's depiction of the Pilate trial presents a double conversation for the Roman governor. Jesus spends much of this trial inside, while Pilate moves back and forth between Jesus inside and the religious authorities outside. The religious authority and the secular authority, but really there is only one authority – it is King Jesus. Pilate finds himself increasingly thwarted in his attempt to release Jesus and frustrate the religious leaders who he already disliked with a passion. As it turned out, they brought in a prejudiced crowd to give the impression of Jewish dislike of Jesus, and they applied the pressure that finally told on Pilate. He condemned Jesus to death by crucifixion.

Death as the Door

Jesus was crucified between two criminals. The soldiers divided up His belongings and all seemed entirely normal in that cruel world of public executions. John tells us that Jesus' mother, along with some other women, was standing near the cross. Crucifixion is a uniquely cruel way to die. The body hangs in such a way that to take a full breath, the condemned has to lift up his weight against the nails that are holding him to the cross. Consequently, it is very difficult for a crucified person to speak.

All four gospels record a total of seven things that Jesus said from the cross. He may have said more. He may very well not have said any more. As the scene is presented in John, we find Jesus speaking to John and to Mary – 'Behold your son. Behold your mother.' Even in the agony of His crucifixion, Jesus is primarily concerned with those He loves. He is ready to prioritise the formation of community in the midst of His own excruciating experience.

All too quickly, John's description of the crucifixion comes to a close as Jesus utters a comment regarding His thirst. After taking the sour wine offered to Him (the cheap stuff the soldiers would have with them), Jesus cries, 'It is finished!' then bows His head and gives up His spirit.

When the Son of Man is lifted up, then you will know that I am. Then I will draw all people to myself. The lifeless form of Jesus' body hung dead on the cross, and people have been drawn to Him ever since.

On the first day of the week, Mary Magdalene came to the tomb. There she met Jesus. At first, she thought He was the gardener and asked where the body of Jesus had been moved. Then she heard His voice say her name and she knew it was her Jesus – He was risen from the dead! His next words were powerful, 'Do not cling to me, for I have not yet ascended to the Father; but go to my brothers and say to them, "I am ascending to my Father and your Father, to my God and your God".' For the first time in the Gospel, Jesus refers to His Father as their Father too. Now the doorway into the family has been opened and all people are truly invited into the glorious fellowship of the Trinity!

An Overwhelming Love

From the Fall of Adam and Eve onwards, every human has been born into the world with a profound incurvature of the soul. We don't have to be taught to love ourselves, for we are all naturals at it. Every moment of every day we will naturally look out for number one. Some will manifest this incurved soul through the pursuit of gross pleasures at the expense of others. Others will manifest this incurved soul through self-righteous efforts that draw praise and commendation from others. The self-love of the fallen human would be impressive if it were not so desperately sad.

What would it take to draw us out of this grip of self, this kingdom of me, and draw us to trust another? The truth is, we think we are the best at loving ourselves. Some will, by their successes in life, be fooled into thinking they are the masters of their own destiny. Others will, in their failures, be fooled into thinking that if circumstances were different, or if they just tried a bit harder, then they would be successful and self-made. Everyone will, irrespective of success or failure, believe that they remain best placed to care for self since nobody loves me as much as I do.

So what would it take to draw us out of this grip of self? The stronger the grip, the more far-reaching the solution must be. What could be more breath-taking than the God who made us, hanging naked and humiliated, arms outstretched, for us?

The cross was a multifaceted event. On the cross Jesus was paying the price for the sin of the world. This was a substitutionary sacrifice to atone for sin. In many of the writings in our New Testament, this is the emphasis. But in John's Gospel, the emphasis is different. On the cross Jesus was obeying the will of His Father, whose love for the world caused Him to send His Son. On the cross, Jesus was drawing all people to Himself.

What would it take to draw us out of our gripping self-love? Sadly, it took the cruel cross of Christ to get our attention and prompt us to believe that maybe God could actually love us more than we love ourselves. In the cross of Christ we glimpse a love that can overwhelm even our great self-love.

Union for Union

We started this book by pondering the eternal union of the Trinity. God the Father and God the Son in perfect union by God the Holy Spirit. The most perfect of relationships – a love that could not be contained. That fountain of love, with that uncontainable spreading goodness, birthed both the creation and the redemption too.

We started section three of this book by pondering the Christmas story. We were astonished that the eternal Son of God would willingly come and enter our world in the most humble of circumstances. In the incarnation, a glorious union took place. It was the union of God and man in the person of Jesus. Fully God, fully man, fully one, forever.

That union made possible the third and final union – the union between the Son of God and redeemed humanity. Jesus knew He was on a marital mission. He knew that He was sent to go to the cross and redeem His bride from out of this fallen and God-hating humanity. Some might see Jesus as the most famous bachelor of all time, but that would be to entirely miss the point. He came to get a wife, and He succeeded. The cross was the ultimate proposal. *I love you this much. Will you marry me?*

The fourth and final section of this book will ponder that divine marriage. We will go into the epistles to ponder the wonder of our union with Christ. Then we will finish with the wedding description of Revelation, where hopefully our journey through the Bible will end with us absolutely lost in wonder.

Part Four

Union with Christ

Him [The Holy Spirit] therefore, I shall send on purpose to be in my room, and to execute my place to you, my bride, spouse, and he shall tell you, if you will listen to him, and not grieve him, nothing but stories of my love.[1]

THOMAS GOODWIN

Not only is the Christian 'in the Spirit' but the Spirit is 'in him'....This is the ultimate doctrine, it is the highest peak of the Christian doctrine of salvation.[2]

D. MARTYN LLOYD-JONES

1. Thomas Goodwin, *The Heart of Christ* (Edinburgh: The Banner of Truth Trust, 2011), p. 19.
2. D. Martyn Lloyd-Jones, *Romans: Exposition of Chapter 8:5-17, The Sons of God* (Edinburgh: The Banner of Truth Trust, 1974), p. 59.

19 **Religion, or Relationship?**

• THE EPISTLE OF JAMES

God's goodness … is near us. It is not a goodness afar off, but God follows us with his goodness in whatsoever condition we be. He applies himself to us, and he hath taken upon him near relations, that he might be near us in goodness. He is a father, and everywhere to maintain us. He is a husband, and everywhere to help. He is a friend, and everywhere to comfort and counsel. So his love it is a near love. Therefore he hath taken upon him the nearest relations, that we may never want [for] God and the testimonies of his love.

And then again this goodness of God, which is the object of love, it is a free goodness, merely from himself; and an

207

overflowing goodness, and an everlasting goodness. It is never drawn dry; he loves us unto life everlasting. He loves us in this world, and follows us with signs of his love in all the parts of us, in body and soul, till he hath brought body and soul to heaven to enjoy himself forever there. These and such like considerations may serve to stir us up to love God, and direct us how to love God.[1]

RICHARD SIBBES

A Christian is not simply 'under' the authority of Jesus. They are not just 'with' the Son of God in spirit. The Christian is 'in' Christ. And you cannot get closer than 'in'.[2]

GLEN SCRIVENER

James was the first New Testament document to be written. As such, it offers us a very early glimpse into the Christianity of the apostolic age. Actually, it offers us three quick and wonderful thoughts to ponder.

First, the fact that Jesus' half-brother became a believer is fantastic. Second, this little epistle is known as the Sermon on the Mount in epistle form – a wonderful resource. Third, even though it is considered the most 'religious' of the New Testament epistles, James invites us into the richness of real relationship with God.

We will dwell on the third thought, but first let's elaborate on the other two.

Jesus' family members did not believe in Him automatically. Actually, they thought He was mad (Mark 3:21).

---

1. Richard Sibbes, 'A Glance of Heaven,' *The Complete Works of Richard Sibbes*, vol. 4 (Edinburgh: The Banner of Truth Trust, 1973), p. 196.
2. Scrivener, *321*, 103.

However, after the Resurrection, at least two of His brothers became true followers of their Messiah-brother. They both wrote a New Testament book (James and Jude), and James became a key leader in the church in Jerusalem. What is so significant about this? Well, if family members were highly sceptical before, then the Resurrection must have been very convincing. It would have been hard to fool doubting family members, but James' place in New Testament history only underlines the truth of the Resurrection and the power of the Gospel.

Acts 12 and 15 show that James, the half-brother of Jesus, was chosen to replace James, the brother of John, as one of the main three leaders in the Jerusalem church (Acts 12:2, 17; 15:13). Barely more than a decade after Jesus returned to heaven, James penned the letter which we now have in our Bibles under his name. It is known as the Sermon on the Mount in epistle form. Why? Because it is full of practical teaching and wisdom, paralleling the teaching of Jesus in the Sermon on the Mount at numerous points throughout the letter. As such, it constitutes a glimpse into early Christianity, and this leads us to the third thought which will dominate this chapter.

James wrote a letter rich in application, but it was not just a manual for life. James wanted to see people who called themselves followers of Jesus actually and fully following Jesus. So James may be the most religious of the New Testament letters – both very Jewish and very practical, but it fully supports the relational nature of the Christian faith as seen in the rest of the New Testament documents. In fact, even in one tiny phrase, it gives us a hint of the marital nature of the believers' relationship with God that should stir worship in our hearts.

Religious, Yes, but Relational Too?

James tells us outright that he is concerned with religion. At the end of the first chapter, he offers a definition of pure and undefiled religion before God. What does God value? 'To visit orphans and widows in their affliction, and to keep oneself unstained from the world' (1:27). Ministries of compassion combined with purposeful personal purity – that is religion. It might appear that chapter 1 focuses on personal purity and the application of the Bible to our lives, and then chapters 2-5 focus on the compassion for others and the resulting unity in the church. Actually, that rigid interpretation appears a little forced. Personal purity, in James, is not just about how we apply the Bible to our lives, it is about how we interact with others in stressful situations. Consequently, as James focuses on more practical issues in chapters 2-5, he continues to inspire believers toward personal purity in the context of their dependence on God and self-giving love toward each other.

Child of a Generous Father

The first chapter launches with encouragement for believers who are facing various kinds of trials and tests. They are encouraged to consider the trials they face as pure joy, and to help them do so they should ask for wisdom from the God who gives generously. The believer should totally trust God for that needed perspective and not rely on their own resources. The believer who stands firm under trial will receive the reward of the crown of life – something God has promised to those who love Him. James presents a generous God who invites humans to love Him – the first hints of a relational faith (1:5-12)

In fact, James goes on to rebuke the idea of blaming God for temptation. Temptation comes from the inner desires of our hearts, not from God; human desire gives birth to sin, which brings death. On the contrary, God is the Father of lights who gives every good gift to His children (1:13-18).

James finishes the first chapter by urging his readers not just to hear God's Word, but to apply it. True religion results in life change – a life of purity and compassion before God, the Father of lights and the generous giver of every perfect gift. True religion reflects the nature of God Himself (1:19-27).

A Friend of God

In his second chapter, James goes after a lack of compassion as seen in the problem of favouritism. It is often in the gathering of a church that this sin can manifest itself. For instance, James highlights the issue of the wealthy being preferred over the needy. But if the believers are gripped by what he calls the royal law, to love their neighbour, then such partiality won't occur. But when it does, even if it seems like a 'lesser' sin, the perpetrator breaks the law nonetheless (2:1-13).

He goes on in the second half of the chapter to show that true faith will always manifest in genuine compassion – a compassion that acts (2:14-26). As an aside, James addresses a group who might oppose what he is writing. Unlike the legalists Paul would later clash with, who believed salvation could be earned by effort, James is countering nominal believers. These were believers in name only; they believed that they could verbally assent to their faith without its having a tangible impact on their lives. So James set about proving that a so-called faith that bears no fruit is no faith at all.

He points to Abraham's act of faith in Genesis 22, and saw the offering of Isaac as the fulfilment of the declaration of faith in Genesis 15. He points also to Rahab who didn't just claim to believe in the God of the Israelites; she acted on that belief. And in the middle of that explanation, he underlines the reality established by Abraham's faith – he became a friend of God.

That is an astonishing statement. To be a child of God is wonderful, but to be considered a friend of God, that is taking it to another level. But there is more …

A Husband?

The third chapter of James points to two key issues in the believer's life: the power of the tongue and division coming from badly sourced wisdom.

The tongue is incredibly hard to tame. But for the believer who is seeking to live a pure life that pleases God, then the tongue will be a critical issue. We cannot tame it ourselves, and unchecked, it will do damage – for from it can come poison and cursing, resulting in division among believers (3:1-12).

Where does division spring from? The tongue plays its part, but the source is bad wisdom (3:13-18). That is, when there is bitter jealousy and selfish ambition in the heart, then this controls the functions of the mind. Whatever wisdom is at work in the mind is not from God, but is devilish. When the heart is captivated by self and antagonistic to others, then it will also influence our actions – 'there will be disorder and every vile practice' (3:16). Bad hearts influence our minds, and our choices, and our relationships with others. On the contrary, wisdom from above bears all the characteristics of selfless Christlikeness – it is pure, peaceable, gentle, open to reason, full of mercy and good fruits, impartial and sincere.

So we come to chapter 4, and James goes after the issue of division even more. What is the cause of division? It is those passions raging within our hearts. Those passions stir us to covet, fight, quarrel and ultimately to destroy others. How does God characterise such self-focused people? 'You adulterous people!' God exclaims, 'Do you not know that friendship with the world is enmity with God?' (4:4) He is not addressing adultery within their human relationships, because he actually writes, 'You adulteresses!' James treats them all as straying wives.

Then to make sure we don't miss the marital language here, James adds, 'He yearns jealously over the spirit that he has made to dwell in us' (4:5). Over the years, scholars have tried to identify the source of this quote, but there is no question that James is thinking of marriage here. Notice the combination of 'adulterous' and 'jealously' with disloyal 'friendship' and the issue of the spirit 'made to dwell in us'. As Douglas Moo puts it, 'James's striking application of the OT imagery of God as the spouse of his people in v. 4 is the key to understanding this verse. Verse 5 explains why flirtation with the world is so serious a matter by bringing to mind the jealousy of the Lord, which demands total, unreserved, unwavering allegiance from the people with whom he has joined himself.'[3]

What James is describing here is the wonder of the Gospel. To be the bride is to have new identity (change in last name, change in legal status, etc.), but also to have a new unity with the groom. God causes His Spirit to dwell in those who are His, and that Spirit is there to unite the believer with God. When that believer reflects worldly values of self-concern and interpersonal squabbling, then they are actually

---

3. Douglas J. Moo, *The Letter of James*, The Pillar New Testament Commentary (Leicester, England: Apollos, 2000), p. 188.

flirting with the world and acting as an enemy of God. God is not passive in all this; He yearns jealously, as any devoted husband would if his wife were flirting with other lovers.

James gives a prescription for this kind of ailing spiritual marriage – it begins with humility (4:6-10). Just as they did at the beginning of the Christian life, so now the erring spouse should embrace humility. God will oppose the proud, but He gives grace to those who recognise their need of Him. By recognising our need for God, we therefore also resist the devil who is trying to draw the believer away from God. The believer should draw near to God – the God who yearns jealously, and who so identifies with His people that He reacts to sin with the response you would expect from a devoted husband.

James describes the contrition you'd expect of an ashamed and adulterous spouse – heart and hand washing, mourning and weeping, sombre reflection (4:8-9). But James' instruction for the squabbling believers is also a glorious invitation for us today. We can draw near to God, confident that He will then draw near to us! What religion can offer that? Reward? Yes. Paradise? Sure. But a God who draws near like a loving spouse to those who are His? Only in Christianity!

So, how should the believers relate to one another? First, without speaking evil against each other. And that humility should stretch into aspects of planning for the future too. God's spouse needs to be dependent on Him, not on their own plans (4:11-17).

The letter concludes with still more instructions which go along with the big themes of the whole letter. Trusting in self by means of wealth is another bad move for the people claiming to be related to God. They should live their lives in light of His coming, not only individually, but paying particular attention to how they treat one another. They shouldn't grumble against one another, but should pray for each other, even anointing the sick with oil. (5:1-20)

James makes a critical point for us to heed as we head into this final section of this book. That is, that our salvation and our relationship with God is never a solo project. Our spirituality will show in our lives – not just in personal purity, but in pure relationships, marked by Christ-like compassion and care. As we move into the next chapters of this book and think about our salvation we will be tempted to treat it all as purely personal. True Christianity can never be solitary. Why? Because the God we are related to is not a solitary being, but a Trinity in community. So as we respond to His love for us, we will manifest the fruit of love and unity in community.

There is more to see, but let's pause and ponder what James has given us – God is not only a generous father and a friend of those who trust in Him, but He is also a God who invites us into a dependent relationship with Him, a relationship the Bible describes as a marriage. We may have wandering eyes, but God wants to woo us back to our union with Him. There is so much more to see in the next chapters, so let's not delay ...

20 Already, Not Yet

• ROMANS

Union with Christ is the central truth of the whole doctrine of salvation. ... There is no truth, therefore, more suited to impart confidence and strength, comfort and joy in the Lord than this one of union with Christ.[1]

JOHN MURRAY

For Paul union with Christ is not fancy but fact – the basic fact, indeed, in Christianity; and the doctrine of imputed righteousness is simply Paul's exposition of the forensic aspect of it.[2]

J. I. PACKER

---

1. John Murray, *Redemption: Accomplished and Applied* (Edinburgh: The Banner of Truth Trust, 1977, originally published in 1955) p. 170-1.
2. J. I. Packer, 'Justification,' in *Evangelical Dictionary of Theology* edited by Walter Elwell (Grand Rapids: Baker, 2001), p. 596.

No condemnation now I dread;
Jesus, and all in Him, is mine!
Alive in Him, my living Head,
And clothed in righteousness Divine,
Bold I approach the eternal throne,
And claim the crown, through Christ my own.[3]

CHARLES WESLEY, *And Can It Be?*

During his third missionary journey, Paul wrote a letter from Corinth that became one of the most loved and revered documents in all of human history – the letter to the Romans. For Christianity this letter has been hugely influential. It is the go-to letter for many of the core truths of the faith. Many of the great heroes of church history were profoundly marked by an encounter with Romans – Augustine of Hippo and Martin Luther are two notable examples.

For many years, Romans was viewed as a presentation of Paul's gospel stripped of any local relevance. That idea has been rejected as students of Romans have recognised more and more how much it was written in a specific context, at a unique moment in time, to a particular group of believers. In the New Testament, the good news from God is always given 'in concrete' – that is, to a specific situation.

The Background of Romans

When Paul wrote Romans, he had not yet been to Rome. However, this does not mean that he was unaware of the situation there. All roads led to Rome and it would have been difficult not to know what was going on at the hub of the empire. Paul knew about the Jewish background believers, as

---

3. Charles Wesley, 'And Can It Be?', Hymn, 1738.

well as the non-Jewish background believers, two groups who constituted the house churches in Rome. Paul knew about the tensions between them. Paul also knew that if the Roman church was to give him the help he needed as he headed on to Spain then it would need to be united and healthy (see Rom. 15:24-28). Paul did not write Romans merely to prove his credibility, but to exert his pastoral influence and bring health to the church.

Paul was also facing a unique moment in his own life. His long-term goal was Spain, but immediately on the horizon for him was a complex aid mission. He was on the way to deliver a gift from Gentile Christians to the Jewish Christians in Jerusalem. This special collection was a practical unification project to ensure unity between the 'traditional' church in Jerusalem and the 'new' churches across the Roman Empire.

Actually, there had been Jews from Rome at Pentecost, so technically the church in Rome was as old as the church in Jerusalem. But even in the course of a quarter of a century, enough time had passed for traditions to set in in Jerusalem and the progress of the Gospel to be perceived as 'new' and somehow separate. But there was only one body of Christ and Paul was risking a lot to make that clear.

So as Paul headed to Jerusalem, he almost certainly wanted to be able to say that while there hadn't been time to add to the collection from the church in Rome, still they had been kept abreast of developments – strengthening by association his message of unity.

The Message in a Nutshell

What the Roman churches needed, and what Paul planned to share in Jerusalem, was the unifying power of the Gospel. In the Gospel there is a revelation of the righteousness of

God, which is given to all who receive God's good gift by faith, both Jews and Gentiles.

Romans is a demonstration of God's faithfulness to promises that were made centuries, even millennia earlier. Jewish and Gentile background believers had nothing to boast about, for they were all equally lost and condemned before God (chapters 1–3). But God gave them both His own righteousness, never based on their merit, but always by faith in Christ (chapters 3–8). So if God's loving gift to the Gentiles is so wonderful, people might ask, what happened to Israel? Did God cast them aside? Paul answers this question next, underlining that they can have assurance of God's love in the present due to God's ongoing faithfulness to His promise plan (chapters 9–11). Finally, Paul gets to his practical application in the final chapters of the book, that the righteousness should be lived out in the tangible spheres of church life, and life in the empire (chapters 12–15). Ultimately, his goal is that the groups within the church should welcome and accept one another (see 15:7-13).

In Romans we can trace the pairing of sin and grace, with God's grace always greater than our sin. We see the depth of the sin problem in the hearts of humanity, and the profound provision of God's loving work through Christ and the Holy Spirit. We see both the profound transformation achieved by the Gospel, but also the present struggle of believers living in anticipation of what still lies ahead …

The Three-Fold Fall

In Romans 8:18-25, Paul describes the tension between present sufferings and future glory. At the moment there is a problem. Actually, since the very beginning the impact of the Fall of Genesis 3 has been felt by every molecule in all of creation. What actually happened that day when Adam and Eve took the forbidden fruit? As we dig into Romans 8:18-25 we gain clarity on what occurred back in Genesis 3.

God had told Adam that on the day he ate of the tree, he would surely die. But the serpent caused Eve to doubt God's Word on this issue … how could she die? After all, the serpent had himself made such an independent choice and he wasn't dead. Since they didn't die that day, obviously God was wrong.

Not so fast. Actually, they did die that day, spiritually. And they also began to die, physically. Here are the three elements of the Fall:

1. ***Spiritual Death*** – In that very moment, when they took that fruit and ate it, something very significant occurred. Genesis 3 marks the moment by stating that they were naked and were ashamed (compare Gen. 2:25 and 3:7). They started to hide, because they were now profoundly self-aware. They started to compete and to blame everyone else, since they were now, in a weird and perverse way, 'gods' – that is, pseudo-gods at the centre of their own little universe. What does it mean that they died spiritually? The standard answer is that they became separated from God. But what does that mean? Was it simply a legal condemnation that separated them from a perfect God? We saw in John 3 (chapter 16), that Jesus viewed post-Fall humanity as needing a new Spiritual birth from above. When they died spiritually, they lost the presence of the Spirit of God binding them to God Himself, and binding them to each other in their human marriage.

2. ***Physical Death*** – They lived on physically for many years, but the sand started falling through the timer that day. Their bodies moved unremittingly toward death.

As a missionary once told my colleague, 'It would be no mercy of God to clothe an immoral soul in an immortal body.' Death was now part of the human narrative, and it has been ever since.

3. ***Creation Death*** – They witnessed the first physical death as God slaughtered animals to provide bloody garments for them. How horrific that must have been for their previously fully sensitive consciences. They were supposed to be the 'image of God' rulers of creation. Now they were witnessing bloodshed and hearing final gasps for the first time. Ever since their sin, the creation itself has been 'subjected to futility' and it is under 'bondage to corruption'. Creation itself groans.

The entrance of sin into this world provoked a groan that still reverberates around creation – every tree, every fish, every bird, and every animal is dying. We ourselves, the image bearers for the life-giving God, walk through life with creaking bodies, groaning as we head toward death. And the worst of it is this, that we cloak our frailty in the false garb of pseudo-divinity. Without the Spirit of God, humans live life as if they are, in fact, mini-gods!

This is a desperate situation, but the Gospel changes the picture entirely!

The Three-Fold Redemption

Actually, the Gospel changes the picture entirely, eventually. Right now, the Gospel changes part of the picture entirely. In Romans 8:18-25, Paul describes the creation groaning in anticipation of a future day when the children of God will be glorified. Not only does the creation groan, but we also groan, as we await our 'adoption as sons, the redemption of our bodies' (v. 23). So if our bodies and creation are still waiting, what has changed? We look forward to that day because we 'have the first fruits of the Spirit'.

The Gospel stirs hope in us because we have received a down-payment, so to speak, the Spirit Himself has come to dwell in us. We now have the first part of the redemption required to overcome the impact of the Fall:

1. ***Spiritual Life Now*** – In the Gospel we have the first fruits of the Spirit. In Ephesians 1:13-14 Paul explains that the believer is sealed with the Spirit. We have the Spirit now, which means we have true, Spiritual, God-given, God-connected life again. In John 17:3, John explained eternal life as 'knowing the one true God, and Jesus Christ whom he has sent'. We know God and Christ by the Spirit who unites us to Christ. The presence of the Spirit is life, and in the Gospel we are very much alive, already!

2. ***Physical Redemption Coming*** – But as you may have noticed, even if you have the Spirit of God in you, your body is still failing. Our backs ache. Common colds can stop us in our tracks. Diseases still kill us. Yet now we have hope that our condition is not ultimately terminal. If we have the Spirit of God in us now, then whatever happens to our bodies, one day we will be able to run and jump again! One day our bodies will be redeemed from the curse of sin and death.

3. ***Creation's Release Coming*** – And so the clock is ticking for creation too. One day the futility of trying to live on a stage of death will be finished. Our world

is like Narnia creaking under the curse of a forever winter, but the presence of the Spirit in the children of God means that a thaw is coming. One day winter will be over and spring will have well and truly sprung for creation itself. We have only glimpsed the wonder of creation up until now. The best is yet to come! As Paul put it, 'I consider that the sufferings of this present time are not worth comparing with the glory that is to be revealed to us.' (Rom. 8:18)

2 Out of 3 Feels Bad

This passage gives us a glimpse into the tension in which we live. If we have trusted Christ for our salvation then we have received the Spirit of God into our lives, melting our hearts with the love of God, stirring our hearts to love Him, and uniting us to Christ right now. We are His! But there is a tension that remains.

The redemption is incomplete. Spiritually (number 1 above) we are redeemed! But for our bodies and for creation (numbers 2 and 3 above), this redemption is still to come. What does that mean for those of us who belong to Christ? We should anticipate tension as long as we are still in this old and dying flesh. When Paul uses the term flesh, he is speaking of our bodies, but also our old way of life, our old habits, our old ways of thinking, our old rebellious and God-hating values. Our flesh has its own set of desires and these are very much opposed to the new inner taste our hearts have for Christ and the things of God. Holiness is now attractive to us, but we still have a well-developed appetite for sin. How can this be? We have two sets of desires at war within.

You probably don't need much convincing that there is a tension between your spiritual appetites and your fleshly desires. That is something we know all too well. I certainly do.

To further understand this tension, let's pull back from Romans 8:18-25 and see the bigger picture. Paul is not simply writing about our legal status and a way God has made to deal with our guilty status before Him. Paul is writing relationally about our union with Christ, even while we remain in this sinful flesh.

Reconciled and Loved

If we follow the argument through from chapter 5, we can trace the relational nature of the Gospel. In light of the justification described in the previous two chapters, we now have peace with God. We were at enmity with God, but now we have been reconciled to God by the death of Christ. The love of God was demonstrated at Calvary when Christ died for us. And the love of God continues to be poured out into our hearts by the Holy Spirit who is also given to us (5:1-11, note especially v. 5).

So there is a partial parallel between Adam, who brought death to all, and Christ, whose death offers life to all. Sin increased, but grace abounded in Christ! (5:12-21) So what does this mean for us? Chapter 6 tells us that we have been baptised into Christ Jesus. We have been immersed into Him, and therefore also into His death. We are united with Christ in the newness of life. Don't reduce this to a mere status change; this is speaking of a true union between us and Christ. (Don't forget, the Spirit of God pours out His love into our hearts now, which speaks of this spiritual union between the believer and Christ!)

Consequently, while our old self still exists and makes lots of noise, we are no longer enslaved to sin as we were before.

We now have newness of life. So we should live for Christ now, not for sin. The passion for sin may still be present in the flesh, but our bodies have a new life and purpose now. So we should present ourselves to God, not to sin. (6:1-14) Since we are not under law any more (that was given to increase sin, not to solve the problem), should we sin freely? Absolutely not. We are no longer slaves to sin, but instead are slaves of righteousness, obedient from the heart. The heart change that comes with the presence of the Spirit means we can live different lives now. (6:15-23)

Let's go back to the tension we feel between our flesh and the Spirit. In chapter 7, Paul offers a famous description of this tug-of-war. He begins with a marital illustration. A woman is only bound to her husband as long as he lives. Once he dies, she is free to marry again. Likewise, the believer is now dead to the law. Why? Because in our union with Christ we have died to the law and we now 'belong to another'. (7:1-6) Paul goes on to describe the already and not yet tension we saw in the three-fold fall and so-far-one-part redemption above. The commandments of God are good and spiritual, but the flesh corrupts the good and so there is tension – 'I do not do what I want, but I do the very thing I hate.' (7:15) In the flesh the picture is very bleak, but the Spirit within us gives us a new set of 'wants' that are perfectly good. We delight in the law of God, but we have in our flesh a different set of desires. So, with Paul, we cry out, 'Wretched man that I am! Who will deliver me from this body of death?' (v. 24). But in our spiritual union with Christ there is hope even as we live in this now-but-not-yet tension, 'Thanks be to God through Jesus Christ our Lord!' (v. 25). Chapter 8 develops that hope.

In chapter 8, we are greeted with amazing news that just keeps on getting better. First, there is no condemnation for those who are in Christ Jesus. Notice the 'in Christ Jesus' and think relationally. We will develop this 'in Christ' theme in the next two chapters – it is the very centre of Paul's Gospel!

Second, we can fulfil the righteous requirement of the law – not in our own strength, but as we set our minds on the things of the Spirit (8:5). We saw a reference to the new way of the Spirit in 7:6, but what is Paul referring to when he writes about setting our minds on the things of the Spirit? How about back in 5:5? The love of God is poured into our hearts by the Spirit. The Spirit is all about the union between God and God, and now, between God and humanity. As we set our minds on to the love of God poured out into our hearts, we can now live righteous lives in response to that love.

Third, and we are only skimming the surface here, not only are we in Christ, but Christ is in us (8:9-10). The fourth piece of good news (and this just keeps on getting better) is that we now are led by the Spirit (8:12-14). Fifth, the Spirit within us stirs us to cry 'Abba! Father!' convincing our spirits that we are children of God (8:15-16). This means that we are heirs of God and fellow heirs with Christ – our brother, or our spouse. (We got into the family both by adoption, and by marriage!)

So, sixth, we can anticipate the glory to come when our bodies also experience the redemption our spirits already know (8:18-25). Seventh, the Spirit helps us to pray when we don't know how to express ourselves to God (8:26-27).

All of this relational wonder adds up to a stirring conclusion. As adopted children of God, as those who are united to Christ by the Spirit – we are in Christ, He is in us – the finale of Romans 8 is a chorus of wonder for us! If God is for us, what enemy need we fear? If He didn't spare

His very own Son, but actually gave Him for us, won't He surely also provide the trivial things we need? So what could ever separate us from God's love in light of all this? Praise God, nothing!

We are going to probe this idea of being 'in Christ' some more. But first, please, be sure to put this book down and at least read Romans 8 before you carry on!

21 In Church and in Christ

• 1 AND 2 CORINTHIANS

True religion is an union of the soul with God, a real participation of the divine nature, the very image of God drawn upon the soul; or in the Apostle's phrase, *it is Christ formed within us.*[1]

HENRY SCOUGAL

The heart of Paul's religion is union with Christ. This, more than any other conception, … is the key which unlocks the secrets of his soul.[2]

JAMES STEWART

---

1. Henry Scougal, *The Life of God in the Soul of Man*, p. 6.
2. James Stewart, *Man in Christ* (1935 reprinted, Vancouver: Regent College, 2002), p.147, in Marcus Peter Johnson, *One With Christ*, p. 20.

As he wrote Romans, Paul had no first-hand experience of the problems in Rome, although he would have been fully aware of them from a distance. Corinth was a different story. Paul was all too familiar with the challenges facing this young church. He knew the church having spent much time there (see Acts 18). In addition, he had received a visit from some people in the church and they had brought a letter containing specific questions. All this added up to a very targeted and practical letter in response (1 Cor.). Following further visits from Paul to Corinth, and a visit from Titus on his behalf, Paul wrote 2 Corinthians.

Paul knew the complexities of the situation in Corinth. But don't miss this: Paul's response to the specific and practical problems in the church at Corinth was thoroughly theological and gospel-centred. He did not simply offer a to-do list for the church, or a quick pragmatic set of suggestions. He gave them gospel-saturated answers that provide profound insight for us (and, in turn, help for our complex and messy local church situations!)

What is the church? In the two epistles to Corinth we have at least four big metaphors for the church. Paul viewed the church as a building (1 Cor. 3:9-11); as the bride of Christ (2 Cor. 11:2); as a body (1 Cor. 12:12-13) and as a temple (1 Cor. 3:16-17; 6:19-20; 2 Cor. 6:14–7:1).

It would be easy to see these metaphors as offering both harder and softer ideas of the church. That is, the harder engineering and architectural view of a building and temple, set off against the softer relational and organic view of a body and the bride. Setting the images against each other like this would be a mistake. All of the images used for the church convey something of the relational bond between Christ and His people, typically in the context of the work of the Spirit.

We Are In Christ

In the introduction of the first epistle, Paul describes how the believers were called by God 'into the fellowship of his Son, Jesus Christ our Lord' (1 Cor. 1:9). To be a Christian is to be in a relationship with Christ. Indeed, as Paul writes at the other end of the epistle, if anyone does not love Christ, then he is not saved, but is hell-bound! (1 Cor. 16:22)

The language Paul uses goes further than just being brought into fellowship with Christ. As we will see, 'the fellowship of Christ' speaks of a kind of communion and togetherness that reflects the relationship of the Trinity. What gives this away? The role of the Holy Spirit. In the rest of the letter Paul goes beyond any idea of a contract-based mutual interaction, to the idea of mutual indwelling. That is, by the Spirit, we are in Christ. And, amazingly, Christ is in us!

Remember, Paul is writing to a messy and worldly church, but he introduces the letter by referring to them being 'sanctified in Christ' (1 Cor. 1:2), and recipients of the grace of God, 'in Christ' (1 Cor. 1:4). Yet even with this present reality, experiencing the enriching work of the Spirit in their midst, still they 'wait for the revealing of Christ' (1 Cor. 1:7). The believers are where they are because of God's will. They can't boast; it is His work. But where are they? They are 'in Christ' (1 Cor. 1:30).

The Role of the Spirit

In the first chapter of 1 Corinthians, Paul raises the issue of divisions within the church congregation. He appeals for them not to follow their favourite apostle, even if it is him, because it was by God's power that they were saved. Paul walks through a powerful presentation of the weakness and foolishness (in human terms) of his own gospel ministry: his message was apparently foolish and weak, not impressive and persuasive (1:18-25) – it wasn't by his stunning preaching that they were saved. No, the message was weak, and in fact, the recipients of the message were typically unimpressive and weak too! (1:26-31) Actually, Paul the messenger was also weak and unimpressive (2:1-5). So what brought these believers into fellowship with Christ if it wasn't the message or the messenger? It was by the work of God.

So having established the apparent foolishness and weakness of the gospel message, Paul then underlines how by the power of God, the wisdom of God is communicated in the Gospel. In 2:6-16, Paul makes it clear that it is the Spirit who makes known what could never have been known otherwise – the plans and thoughts of God Himself. What, specifically, does the Spirit do? He searches the depths of the thoughts of God. He is the one who knows God intimately and communicates Him ... not just to the Son, but here it is clear that the Spirit does so for us too!

We tend to think of someone as being 'spiritual' if they have some developed personal capacity for things beyond normal life – sort of a higher functioning of their soul. Paul knows nothing of that idea. For Paul, the language of being spiritual means to have received something from outside of ourselves – specifically, the Spirit of God Himself. It is not possible to be spiritual without the Holy Spirit. It is the Spirit who stirs, who moves, and who transforms.

Because the Spirit of God is given to those who are His, this means that we have the 'mind of Christ' communicated to us by the Spirit. If this is what Paul means by being called into the fellowship of Christ, then he must be thinking of something so much richer than a traditional church 'fellowship tea' with its finger foods and polite chit chat! Our fellowship with Christ is based on our being in Him, and having the Spirit of God who searches the depths of Christ and reveals Him to us. Not only are we in Christ, but also …

Christ Is In Us: the Church as God's Temple

Christ in us is exactly where Paul goes next in his letter. In chapter 3, he begins to address the Corinthians' immaturity. The Corinthians thought they were mature, but actually they were very childish; their cliques and apostle-affiliations proved as much. Actually, *all* the apostles were co-farming the field with God, and co-building the building with God. 'I planted, Apollos watered, but God gave the growth.' (1 Cor. 3:6) By verse 9, Paul drops the brief horticultural metaphor to develop the architectural one (see 3:5-15). This idea of the church being a building then becomes even more specific – the church is a temple.

(This is not referring to the later development of the church owning a building and becoming identified with it, but it refers to the people themselves actually being a building.)

Why does Paul specifically use the image of a temple? Isn't this confusing the old religion of Israel with new Christianity? Not necessarily. What did the Jews think of when they thought of the temple? A building set apart for rituals and ceremonies? Perhaps, but more likely they would celebrate the uniqueness of their temple as the place where God chose to dwell. The God of the Hebrew Scriptures is a God who has always chosen to dwell in the midst of His undeserving people. When the tabernacle was made, and again when Solomon's temple was dedicated, the presence of God in the form of the shekinah glory came in a special way into the Holy of Holies. This was the rich reality of the Jewish temple, and Paul is clearly thinking along the same lines here:

> Do you not know that you are God's temple and that God's Spirit dwells in you? If anyone destroys God's temple, God will destroy him. For God's temple is holy, and you are that temple. (1 Cor. 3:16-17, see also Acts 2 and the fiery presence of God at the dedication of this new temple at Pentecost!)

As Paul moves beyond the issue of divisions in the church, he focuses in on reports regarding the unholiness of the church in chapters 5 and 6. There is a case of immorality that had been reported to him that even the pagan culture would have been shocked by. But the church there, with their confused view of their own maturity and spirituality were actually celebrating how liberated they were! Furthermore, they were taking each other to court to settle disputes, which looked terrible to the watching world. And finally, in the second half of chapter 6, they were treating their bodies as irrelevant to their spirituality.

In this last section of Paul's responses to reports, he comes back to the idea of the church being a temple of the Holy Spirit. They were celebrating their freedom in the Gospel by separating their spiritual identity from their physical behaviour. There were several reasons for this, including a culturally influenced idea of separating the physical realm from the spiritual realm, and a sense of already having arrived at spiritual maturity. They were wrong on both counts. The physical realm is intimately tied to the spiritual, and they were neither spiritual nor mature!

Specifically, they were messing around with prostitutes. But Paul reminded them, in no uncertain terms, that their bodies were meant for the Lord, not for personal pleasure pursuits. More than that, how could they take their physical bodies, which were members of the body of Christ, and unite them with the physical members of a prostitute? After all, physical union was part of the original marriage design for a one-flesh relationship. Uniting with a prostitute physically was to do something profoundly spiritual and completely inappropriate. They surely wouldn't take Christ to a prostitute, and yet they were doing that by visiting prostitutes themselves!

Was Paul really identifying the horizontal relationship (believer with prostitute) as a marital connection? Yes, he quotes from Genesis 2:24 to make his point – 'the two will become one flesh.' (1 Cor. 6:16) And what does he say about the vertical relationship? In the very next verse he equates that with a marital connection – 'he who is joined to the Lord becomes one spirit with him.' (1 Cor. 6:17) The Christian is not just bound to Christ by some sort of legal arrangement, or contractual affiliation … it is a marriage. Just to make this clear, Paul reinforces his point – 'do you not know that your body is a temple of the Holy Spirit within you ..?'. (1 Cor. 6:19)

While the context may seem very foreign to us, the theology presented in this section shows that Paul viewed the Christian relationship with Christ to be more than a legal arrangement – it was a one-spirit marital union! This had massive implications for their view of church life, of spiritual maturity, and of personal behaviour, as Paul was spelling out for them in his letter. Union with Christ brings a very high moral standard into play for the believer today too – for by our actions we are taking Christ into each situation.

Marriage

Paul moves from responding to reports (chapters 1–6), to responses to specific questions that were sent to him by letter (chapters 7–15). The first question he addresses relates to issues surrounding marriage. Without getting into all the details, Paul's response in chapter 7 reveals a high view of marriage but also of singleness (a state which allows for undistracted devotion to Christ – see 7:32-35).

Jumping into the second letter to the Corinthians, Paul begins with an extended section on the New Covenant and the glorious inside-to-out ministry of the Spirit at work in this new era. The Spirit shines the glory of God's Trinitarian delight into the hearts of believers (see 4:6). Paul then returns to the image of the temple.

Paul wanted the Corinthians to be responsive to the grace of God. He knew that 'unequally yoked' business relationships would draw them away from their 'temple' purpose and purity – i.e. to be definitively God's set apart people, having God as their father. In this temple section, 2 Cor. 6:14–7:1, Paul again is incredulous that they would try to blend or bond light in fellowship with darkness.

The marital theme becomes overt when we arrive in chapter 11. By this stage, Paul is addressing the frustrating critique he had been receiving from false apostles. As he is preparing to counter their claims with some 'foolish boasting' of his own, he gives this glimpse into his own, and God's heart, for the Corinthians:

> For I feel a divine jealousy for you, since I betrothed you to one husband, to present you as a pure virgin to Christ. (2 Cor. 11:2)

This building which is a temple, indwelt by the Spirit of God; and this body of Christ which is connected to Christ, the head; is, in fact, the bride of Christ. Paul writes that he betrothed her to one husband. His goal was to present her as a pure virgin to Christ. The language could not be any more marital than this. In fact, he immediately goes back to the Garden of Eden:

> But I am afraid that as the serpent deceived Eve by his cunning, your thoughts will be led astray from a sincere and pure devotion to Christ. (2 Cor. 11:3)

The issue for Eve, and for the Corinthians, was that the enemy always wants to draw devotion away from Christ. Paul was fearful that this would happen under the influence of the false apostles trying to gain a following in Corinth.

So as Paul comes to the end of the second epistle, we find him urging the Corinthians to examine themselves to see whether they are actually in the faith. He is concerned that their immorality and susceptibility to false teaching may be revealing that actually they are not 'in the faith'. Immediately he encourages the Corinthians to look at the same truth from the other side, 'Or do you not realise this about yourselves, that Jesus Christ is in you?' (13:5)

This chapter has barely scratched the surface of the complex issues in the church at Corinth. But throughout both letters, Paul points to the theological foundations of their salvation – their union with Christ. Being in Christ meant that they were the body of Christ. Having Christ in them, by the Spirit, meant that they were a temple of the Holy Spirit. Them in Christ and Christ in them meant that they were the bride of Christ. The theology of union here is so rich. So it is fitting for Paul to conclude with a very famous verse:

> The grace of the Lord Jesus Christ and the love of God and the fellowship of the Holy Spirit be with you all. (2 Cor. 13:14)

Here is the fellowship of the Trinity, the grace coming from the Son, and the love given by the Father, which is experienced in the fellowship with Father and Son by the Holy Spirit. This is the great privilege of the believer.

22 Union with the Trinity

• EPHESIANS

But faith must be taught correctly, namely that by it you are so cemented to Christ that He and you are as one person, which cannot be separated but remains attached to Him forever and declares: 'I am as Christ.' And Christ, in turn, says: 'I am as the sinner who is attached to me and I to him. For by faith we are joined together into one flesh and bone.' Thus Ephesians 5:30 says: 'We are members of the body of Christ, of his flesh and bones,' in such a way that faith couples Christ and me more intimately than a husband is coupled to his wife.[1]

MARTIN LUTHER

1. Martin Luther, 'Lectures on Galatians,' in *Luther's Works*, 55 vols., gen.ed. Jaroslav Pelikan (St Louis: Concordia; Philadelphia: Fortress Press, 1955-1975), Vol. 26, p. 168.

The Gospel is a doctrine of mysteries. O what mysteries are here! The Head in heaven, the members on earth, yet really united! Christ in the believer, living in him, walking in him: and the believer dwelling in God, putting on the Lord Jesus, eating his flesh and drinking his blood! This makes the saints a mystery to the world, yea, a mystery to themselves.[2]

THOMAS BOSTON

I am crucified with Christ,
And the cross hath set me free;
I have ris'n again with Christ,
And He lives and reigns in me.

This the secret of the holy,
Not our holiness, but Him;
O Lord! empty us and fill us,
With Thy fulness to the brim.[3]

A. B. SIMPSON
I Am Crucified With Christ

At the very beginning of the Bible, at the climax of the creation account, God purposed that man should leave his father and mother and be united to his wife. In Ephesians 5:31-32, we finally discover that God was speaking of something more than human marriage – He was speaking of Christ and the church. Therefore this book would be incomplete without looking at the theme of marriage and union in Ephesians. We could go straight to the final section of chapter 5, the great

---

2. Thomas Boston, *Human Nature in Its Fourfold State* (Carlisle, PA: The Banner of Truth Trust, 1964; repr., 1989), p. 257.

3. A. B. Simpson, 'I Am Crucified With Christ', Hymn.

marriage section, but that would be to miss several chapters of relevant material. Let's orient ourselves to its context and then quickly walk through the whole letter. We will look at the marriage section, I promise.

Christianity 101

Ephesians has some of the richest theology of the New Testament, but it is really a beginner's course in Christianity. Paul had visited Ephesus during his second and third missionary journeys. He had spent more time in ministry there than any other stop on his travels. Why? Because Ephesus was the hub of the region. By basing his ministry there, everyone in Asia Minor was able to hear the word of the Lord (see Acts 19:10).

In fact, the impact of his ministry was so profound, that two generations later, the governor of neighbouring Bithynia referred to the gradual return of people to the pagan temples in a letter to the emperor (Pliny the Younger to Emperor Trajan ca. A.D. 112). In Paul's day, thousands had gathered to defend the honour of their goddess Artemis (see Acts 19:23-41), but the gospel obviously struck deep in the hearts of many thousands during his years in Ephesus.

Paul connected with the Ephesian elders again on his way back to Jerusalem at the end of the third journey (Acts 20:15-38). Tychicus and Trophimus, representatives from the Asian region, accompanied him on this trip. During his days in Jerusalem, some locals saw Paul in the temple and assumed that he had taken Trophimus with him (obviously they were known to be close), and since Trophimus was a Gentile, Paul got into very hot water (Acts 20:4; 21:29). Arrested and held for trial, Paul spent the next two years in a prison cell. Then, when it was clear that the

Jews intended to kill him, Paul appealed to Caesar and got an expenses paid trip to Rome to have Caesar hear his case. A further two years in prison in Rome provided the window for Paul to write this and the other so-called 'Prison Epistles' (Colossians, Philippians and Philemon).

Paul had been blamed for a sin supposedly committed by Trophimus, a believer from the Ephesians' own region. Now the great apostle had spent almost four years in prison. Surely the Ephesians felt some discouragement at all this. But Paul wanted them to be encouraged. In fact, he wanted them to get a clear view of this Christian faith that made sense of all the suffering. So Paul wrote to the Ephesians. Actually, he wrote to the whole region. Many scholars believe that Paul wrote a circular letter that would have started in Ephesus, but then would have been copied and passed on to the other churches in the region. He wanted the whole region to have their foundations solidly built, even in his absence.

The Trinity and the Church

Ephesians reveals much about the Trinity. It starts with a description of each member of the Trinity participating in our salvation. The Father lovingly chose us and sent His Son to redeem us by His blood. The Father's plan continued as He sent the Holy Spirit to seal His purchased people (1:3-14). Through the Son and by the Spirit, the Father has blessed us with every spiritual blessing. The letter continues in this vein. The Father's lavish love and purposeful initiative marks Him out as the great focal point of the letter. In the early chapters of the letter, the Father is referred to more times than even Christ Himself.

Ephesians also reveals much about the church. The church is the bride of Christ, a body united in Christ to work out God's purposes in the world. In fact, the great theme of the letter turns out to be the union of Christ and His people, the church. Paul prays for them to come to know God more: the certain expectation created by His calling, the glorious inheritance that He considers the church to be, and the amazing power of God that is toward those who believe in Him (1:15-23). In chapter two, Paul points out that God didn't just raise Christ from the dead, He also raised the Ephesians to new life: they were dead, but by God's great mercy, they have also been raised and seated with Christ (2:1-10). Finally, Paul gets to the great theme that will dominate the letter …

The New Temple and Union with Christ

The letter began with God's intent to present us holy and blameless before Him (see 1:4), which resonates with the same idea presented later in the marriage section (see 5:27). Could it be that marriage is in Paul's mind from the very beginning of the letter? Certainly once the temple image starts to weave through the letter, we actually have a complex and subtle marriage picture in view. How does the temple image relate to the idea of marriage, and how does it show up in the letter? Marriage is where two people are bound together by the Spirit bonding them through the concept of mutual indwelling (two people so united they become one). The temple is a glorious picture of God's presence dwelling in the midst of His people. Combine this with the idea of believers being 'in Christ' (Christ dwelling in us by His Spirit) and now we have a composite theme that is very 'marital' in its force.

Where does the temple theme show up? In the second half of chapter 2. Here Paul focuses in on the wonder of the Gospel bringing people together in the church. The local context in Asia Minor meant that the church contained both Jewish and Gentile background believers, and they needed to be united. So Christ came and preached peace to those who were near and those who were far off, a message that had since been brought to Asia Minor. Through His work, Christ brought near those who had been far off, so that all people might have access in one Spirit to the Father. He described this new construction as a holy temple – a dwelling place for God by the Spirit. (See Eph. 2:13-22 especially.)

I remember sitting in a coffee shop with my friend, Mark Stirling, when he invited me to look up Zechariah 6 to see the background to Ephesians 2. There, from verse 9, it speaks of the coming Priest-King, whose name is Joshua (which would be Jesus in the New Testament language), who would build a temple, preaching peace to those far off.

What does this mean? Paul's letter to the Ephesians is gripped by this image of a new temple that Christ is building. And what is the significance of the temple here? It is the dwelling place of God. It is a place, made up of people, where the Spirit of God is fully at home. Do you remember the 'in Christ' and Christ 'in us,' idea that we saw in Romans and Corinthians? Well, in Ephesians Paul really goes for it. Almost forty times he refers to our being 'in Christ' or 'in Him'. And with this temple image, by the Spirit, He is in us! Just as God dwelled in the temple in Israel, He now dwells in us! We are His temple! (In Ephesians Paul is not thinking of us as individuals being the temple, but together we are the one temple that Christ is building.)

We too easily think of the temple as a mere building – a structure to protect people from the rain as they do their religious activities. But the temple meant so much more than that. In the region of Ephesus they knew what their temple looked like – an impressive structure functioning as a shrine, where a pagan deity was supposedly present.

For the believers who were aware of their Old Testament, the temple was the unique feature that distinguished Jerusalem from all other places. Sure, if you were Jewish you could live in Alexandria with its great library, or in Rome with its many luxuries. But really, why would you live anywhere but Jerusalem? After all, the temple was there. God chose to dwell in their midst, by His Spirit, in the temple. He wanted to be close to His people. So now, with this new temple made by Christ, which is the church, the true God would be very close to His people – He would be in them!

Tracing the Temple-Union Motif

In chapter 3, Paul goes on a digression before returning to the temple theme. The digression comes as he mentions his prisoner status in verse 1. He is about to pray for them again, but the mention of his prisoner status causes him to explain what it meant for him to be a prisoner on their behalf. Eventually, after one of the most glorious and rich digressions in the Bible, he finally gets to his point – his sufferings are an indication of their glory (3:13). He truly was a prisoner for their sake. (Remember Trophimus? The Ephesians probably felt like it was their fault that Paul was in prison, but Paul would have none of that. He did not want them discouraged about this.)

So in this digression in chapter 3, he explains how God had made known to him the mystery – that formerly secret truth that was now revealed to him, concerning Christ. This secret now revealed was that, in Christ, Gentiles were welcomed as fully equal members of the body – Gentiles didn't need to become Jewish to come to God! So God had given Paul His grace to preach the unsearchable riches of Christ in order that people could know God's great plan. This new entity, *the church*, was God's great plan to make His multi-coloured and complex wisdom known to everyone – not just on earth, but in the heavenly realms too. In Christ, this new body, the church, can boldly access the Father! (3:12)

In verse 14, Paul is able to leave the digression and get back to his prayer. What did he pray for them? That they would be strengthened with power through His Spirit in their inner being (God in us), so that Christ would make Himself at home in their hearts (God in us), so they could grasp the full dimensions – the breadth, the length, the height, the depth ... Of what? Paul is not explicit about what he is describing here. And naturally we might ask why are there four dimensions and not three?

Some translations make this read more smoothly by determining for the reader that these are the dimensions of Christ's love. In a certain sense, this is not wrong. But it does obscure Paul's thought a little. He seems to be coming back to the new temple image again – these are the dimensions of the dwelling for the Spirit of God, whose presence both brings and communicates Christ's love for us. The temple has three dimensions, plus the foundation already referred to in 2:20. To be built into the temple of God – this is what it is to be filled with all the fullness of God!

We the church are in Christ, and in this new temple, His Spirit is dwelling in us, which means we are united to Christ. The force of the temple union motif is strong here. It continues ...

In chapter 4, Paul transitions from the wonder of the church's calling in Christ, to their walking in a manner worthy of that calling. First order of business? Unity. They are to be united with each other. And even though that unity implies togetherness, it does not negate individuality, because Christ gave gifts to each one for the building up of the body of Christ. This temple, the body of Christ, is to grow up as each part plays its role in the healthy functioning of the church as a whole (4:1-16).

The Gospel had truly transformed the Ephesian believers. They were no longer to walk as unbelieving Gentiles do, with their broken thinking controlled by their hardened hearts. The believers had now encountered Christ and 'learned Christ'. (This is a unique use of the verb 'to learn' – it is always used of learning a subject; only here it is used of learning a person – this is so personal and relational!) Having learned Christ, their thinking is changed, and so is their new set of truly righteous and holy behaviours.

What does that transformation look like? In 4:25-32, Paul shows the impact of learning Christ as it progressively cleanses a life. It influences the way they speak, how they respond to anger, and the nature of generosity. Then he drives deeper, showing the deeper impact of the Gospel in each of these areas – not only are they to speak the truth, but they should only speak words that give grace and build up. Not only are they to deal with anger when provoked, but they are to purge all forms of inappropriate divisive anger from their lives. Not only are they to earn money in order to give it away, but they are to give forgiveness, which is often even harder!

Notice how Paul sums up this set of instructions in 5:1-2. They are to walk in love as beloved children. Having been loved by God, they should now love others, which will show in their speech, their responses, and their generosity. But notice particularly how this smells in a community. Smells? In 5:2 Paul uses the language of a fragrant offering and sacrifice. When we love one another in the church, we give off an aroma. We start to smell like Christ. And the imagery used – fragrant offering and sacrifice – this is imagery from the temple. As we love one another in the church, we give off a scent that is like the fragrance of Christ's offering of Himself to God.

American dramatist, Eugene O'Neill, once said that you cannot make a marble temple out of a mixture of mud and manure. But Christ is doing exactly that! We know how much we stink, and yet, even while still in process, Christ is making us into a wonderful marble temple filled with the smell of Christ's loving selflessness! We may not notice this, and we may be all too aware of the manure factor in our church community and in our own life. But when we love one another, the distinctive fragrance of Christ fills us, His new temple!

Paul goes on in chapter 5 to talk about purity and walking in the light. In verses 15-21, Paul writes about wise living and how we should not be filled with wine, but with the Spirit. We tend to take this as an instruction to us as individuals. That is, I must personally be filled with the Spirit. But what if he is still thinking corporately? Then this temple needs to be filled with the Spirit of God, since as a body of believers, we are being built into a dwelling place for God. The theme continues! And how does it look to be filled with the Spirit as a church body? Believers will speak to one another with psalms, hymns and spiritual songs … that makes sense since this temple is to be a place of worship!

As he introduces the idea of submitting to one another in 5:21, so he comes to the great marriage section (5:22-33).

A sudden change of subject? Not really, not if he has been talking of union by means of the temple image since chapter 2. Paul starts by instructing wives to submit to their husbands since the husband is the head of the wife just as Christ is the head of the church. And unlike many in our culture, we don't have to be afraid of the word 'submission'. Biblical submission has nothing to do with inferiority or harsh domination. In reality, Christ Himself submitted to His Father because of love. They are both equal in value, but they had different roles. Christ's submission was in the context of an intimate loving relationship. So it should be in a healthy human marriage. After instructing the wives, then Paul gives instruction to husbands to love their wives just like Christ loved the church – giving Himself up for her, cleansing her, nourishing and cherishing her. Paul continually points out the parallels to Christ who does all this and more for His bride. And then he quotes Genesis:

> 'Therefore a man shall leave his father and mother and hold fast to his wife, and the two shall become one flesh.' (Gen. 2:24)

And it turns out that this was a secret that is now revealed – he was speaking about Christ and the church! (5:32) Could it be that God's plan from the very beginning has been to call out a bride for His own Son? Actually, according to Ephesians, the plan points to calling out a people who could be built into a new temple – a dwelling place for God that would be filled with the Spirit, even as they themselves are also in Christ. Him in us, and us in Him. This is marital language – and it seems to be the unifying theme of the whole epistle.

23 Wedding Anticipations

• 1 JOHN AND REVELATION 1–3

The Spirit of Christ conforms the spouse to be like the husband, and the members to be like the head.[1]

RICHARD SIBBES

The marriage union betwixt Christ and you is more than a bare notion or apprehension of your mind; for it is a special, spiritual, and real union: it is an union betwixt the nature of Christ, God and man, and you.[2]

EDWARD FISHER

---

1. Richard Sibbes, *Works* vol. 1, p. 23.
2. Edward Fisher, *The Marrow of Modern Divinity,* p. 166.

When Christians define themselves by something other than Christ, they poison the air all round. When they crave power and popularity and they get it, they become pompous, patronizing, or simply bullies. And when they don't get it they become bitter, apathetic or prickly. Whether flushed by success or burnt by lack of it, both have cared too much for the wrong thing. Defining themselves by something other than Christ, they become like something other than Christ. Ugly.

Our union with Christ thus has deep plough-work to do in our hearts. It automatically and immediately gives us a new *status*, but for that status and identity to be *felt* to be the deepest truth about ourselves is radical, ongoing business. That is the primary identity of the believer, though, and the only foundation for truly Christian living. For our health, our joy and fellowship, then, we must take up arms against the insidious idea that we have any identity – background, ability or status – more basic than that of sharing the Son's own life together before the Father.[3]

MICHAEL REEVES

We have looked at several of Paul's letters. Even though we should be visiting Colossians for more of the same glorious union theme, we need to return to John's writing to finish our journey through the Bible. Paul and John have their different emphases, but those emphases significantly overlap. For instance, Paul makes much of our being adopted (see Romans 8 and Galatians 4, for example), but John seems to emphasise our being born again into the family of God

---

3. Michael Reeves, *Christ Our Life* (Milton Keynes: Paternoster, 2014), p. 83-84.

(see John 3, for example). These seem to be different themes; after all, adoption is such a legal approach to accessing a family, whereas birth is much more organic. But when we look carefully we find that both writers make much of the initiative of God, the love of God, and the relational bond that is created by the Spirit as we join the family. There is no writer in the New Testament that presents a purely legal or contractual version of salvation. Union is never just a change in status. Our new life in the family of God is always described in warm, relational terms.

We have enjoyed looking at Paul's emphasis on our union with Christ. Being 'in Christ' is Paul's great overarching theme. In John's gospel we saw themes like 'I in you and you in me' as well as 'abiding in Christ' and others. Again, there is great overlap between the two. Indeed, a really strong case can be made that union with Christ is the great theme of the Bible as it describes God's great salvation plan. His goal was to bring us into His family and unite us with Him!

Our being united with Christ includes the legal aspect of justification, the relational aspect of reconciliation, the familial aspects of adoption and regeneration, the transformational aspects of sanctification.

As we come to the conclusion of this book, it is fitting that we return to the writings of John since he was given the privilege of writing the last book of the Bible. Before we get to the end of the story, let's visit his first epistle.

Wedding Anticipation in 1 John

John lived for a generation beyond his fellow apostles. We tend to think of him as an aged apostle exiled on Patmos, but he was active up until the end of his life. For many years, John was involved in the nitty-gritty of local church life in

Ephesus. First John was written to an unnamed church that had endured a split. Some people had left the church claiming to have a special knowledge of God's will and were trying to recruit others to leave with them. John wrote this letter to confront the false teachers and to reassure the faithful believers of the certainty of their standing with God. Their faith was genuine: they were walking in the light, which meant their lives reflected the pure character of God. And they were walking in the love of God, by the Spirit who was within them. They loved the truth and they loved each other.

Fellowship with the Trinity

In the first chapter of 1 John, John launched with a defence of true Christianity based on the reality of the Incarnation – Jesus truly did become a man, and John knew Him personally. Now, all these years later, John's greatest joy would come from the believers enjoying fellowship with the Father and with His Son. The goal of John's ministry was that others would enjoy close fellowship with the Trinity! (1:1-4)

Since God is light, John writes that people who claim to have fellowship and communion with God while living in darkness, must be lying. On the other hand, those who walk in the light can know the amazing truth that sinners can have fellowship with God and with one another, all because the blood of Jesus cleanses us. (1:7) Yet John knew that the believers would feel insecure because of sin in their lives. So he pointed them to the righteous Christ who advocates for them before the Father. Jesus is the solution to the sin problem. (1:5–2:6)

The great commandment of Jesus was that believers should love one another. John encouraged his readers by telling them that their lives were indeed marked by mutual and growing love. Implicitly, those who had left the church were not loving. The false teachers were obviously also denying the incarnation in some way, because John addresses that issue at the end of the second chapter. The Word of God was abiding in the true believers, so that they too were abiding in the Son and in the Father. Here is that mutual indwelling idea that John developed in his gospel. Christ was in them by His word, so they did not need any specially anointed teacher; the Bible itself was sufficient. (2:7-27)

John continues with the idea of abiding in Christ, while anticipating His appearing. Since they were walking in the light, they could await His coming with confident anticipation. At this point he blends the salvation images. They are to rest in Christ because they have been born of God's love. As God's children (who are waiting for Christ), they will naturally purify themselves while they wait, because Christ Himself is pure. This passage seems to combine the image of a bride eagerly awaiting her beloved, and a child sharing in the DNA of its parents – John couldn't be much more relational! (2:28–3:3)

Referring to the false teachers, John writes that those who demonstrate a lack of that godly DNA probably don't have any! They are not in the family. The two groups of people evidenced which family they were in by who they resembled. (3:4-10)

Abiding in Love, in Christ

At this point, John switches from focusing on righteous living to love as his main emphasis. Even though the believers would be hated by the world, their lives would be characterised by love for each other, because they were gripped by Christ's self-sacrificing love. They were abiding in God, and God in them, and they knew this by the Spirit that united them with Him! (3:11-24)

John then contrasts the Spirit that is in the believers with the many spirits that were around. The true Spirit always points to the wonder of Christ and His incarnation. Every spirit that doesn't treat Christ as everything is on the other side, the anti-Christ side. (4:1-6)

Now John gets to the heart of the second half of the book – God is love, and that reality will permeate His people. Just as we can test for paternity via DNA samples and legal background checks, so we can do the simple look-a-like test. ('He is the spitting image of his Dad!') This works for believers too. True believers resemble their loving God! And when we do love one another, it is because God is abiding in us by His Spirit – this is the true union of a believer with God! Several times John underlines that God is abiding in His people and they in Him; the main characteristic of that relationship is love because that is what defines God's identity and relationships. (4:7-21)

So John comes to the end of his letter. He summarises the simple connection between loving God and obeying His command to love. As they trust God, they will overcome the antagonism of the world against them. True Christianity is not about some secret knowledge, but about relational knowledge – knowing Christ which results in love for others. God wants us to know Christ, and to realise that we are in Christ. This is union with Christ, in John's language! (5:1-21)

Wedding Preparation in Revelation

John's final written document was different from his Gospel and his letters. It contained some letters, but also had some apocalyptic features, although he described it as a prophecy.

While some will obsessively focus on the book of Revelation, many tend to avoid it. This is a real shame, since the end of the great story of history, and the great wedding, are such a thrill to ponder.

Revelation ties together loose ends and brings the Bible to a stunning close. God will ultimately tie together the great loose ends of sin and death, of rebellion and questions of God's goodness toward humanity, His right to rule, and His character. It will bring us back to the very beginning, to the Tree of Life and to a sin-free world. But before we go there, let's take a few minutes to examine Jesus' letters to His bride, the church.

John, the beloved disciple, was an old man with fond memories of the Lord he loved. It is hard to imagine how John must have felt, after six decades had passed, to then see the risen Christ again! John saw Jesus dressed in heavenly splendour, resembling the Ancient of Days of Daniel 7 – impressive, majestic, in charge.

The impact on John was overwhelming. John fell at the feet of Christ as if he had died, such was the splendour of the glorified Christ. But Christ calmed his fear and called him to his last privilege during his earthly life – to write the revelation of Jesus Christ for the benefit of the church, including the seven letters to seven particular churches we find in Revelation 2–3.

Jesus' Letter Template

The seven letters from Jesus to the seven churches in Asia Minor follow a clear pattern. It is fairly easy to spot the pattern, but still many miss a key feature of how they work. Each letter begins with a description of Christ, followed by comments about the church (sometimes good, sometimes bad, but usually both), there is a reference to receptive people hearing what the Spirit is communicating with the churches, and there is a promise to the overcomer described at the end.

Who is the conqueror or overcomer? Some people will read these letters and get the impression that the promise is only offered to some kind of super-charged Christian. But, how has John used the language of overcoming in his writing? In his letter he states that it is our faith that overcomes the world (1 John 5:4-5). The overcomer is a normal believer who trusts Christ and therefore endures whatever trials they face in this life. So the promise is not something that is earned, but a motivation for the believer facing the struggle at hand. By faith in Christ all true Christians will be overcomers!

So what do people often miss in these seven letters? Is it some elaborate scheme to tie the seven letters to seven ages of church history (and typically, to make our generation the Laodicean church?) No. We are told to hear the message to all seven churches, not just one. Here's what people often miss – the three big elements in each letter are all tied together. That is, the description of Christ, the comments to the church, and the promise to the overcomer, form one coherent message to the reader.

When we ponder the details of each letter and start to see the connection between these three elements, then the letter will start to stir us in the present. That is often how future-focused content works – it impacts our present living.

John's description of Christ in the first chapter is absolutely breathtaking. Jesus is the Alpha and the Omega, the one who has authority over death and judgment, the ruler of the kings of the earth. He is the Almighty! (1:4-20) Yet in the letters that follow this description, we find that without losing that authority and majesty, Jesus exhibits a relational tenderness that is equally breathtaking. Revelation lifts our eyes to Christ in both His majesty and His tenderness, so that our hearts will beat faster in anticipation of our great wedding to come!

Let's sample the impact of a couple of the seven letters:

Love & Fellowship – Letter to Ephesus (2:1-7)

When Paul met the elders from Ephesus in Acts 20 he warned them about the danger of false teachers who would come in and do damage to the church. Evidently they heeded his warning, because now, a generation later, Jesus commends the Ephesian church for its discernment and determination. This was a strong church in many ways, but what had gone wrong? They had left behind their first love for Christ. They had become a church that was diligent, dutiful, disciplined and determined, but they weren't truly devoted to their groom. (2:2-4)

The description of Christ at the start of the letter to Ephesus portrays Him moving intimately in and out among the churches, holding their leaders in His right hand. He is certainly close to them. He cares. He is near. (2:1)

And the promise to the overcomer? Access to the tree of life, and John makes clear where that tree is located – in the garden of God. Their hearts were being drawn forward to the future privilege of walking with God in the cool of the day, of being in that place that spoke of unfettered devotion to God and close fellowship with Him. (2:7)

So if Christ is close to them and concerned about them, one who is moving intimately among the churches ... If the future will be marked by evening walks with God in the future Eden ... And since Christ pointed out their waning love for Him ... Then the whole letter adds up to an invitation to draw closer to Christ in the present, to enjoy that intimacy now in anticipation of the face to face fellowship still to come.

If only we had the space to trace the theme of life and death in the letter to Smyrna, the suffering church. Or the admonition toward discernment and non-compromise written to Pergamum, the compromised church. Or the idea of judgment and Christ's rule that will be shared with believers, written to the sinning church at Thyatira. Or we could ponder the issue of reputation written to Sardis, the hypocritical church. Or we could look at the themes of trials and security written to Philadelphia, the tested church.

But let's just look at the last letter a little more closely:

Intimacy & Sharing – The Letter to Laodicea (3:14-21)

Paul's letter to the Colossians included an instruction for them to read the letter to the Laodiceans (Col. 4:16). Many scholars believe Ephesians was actually a circular letter that would have travelled through all seven of these churches, with the last one being Laodicea. Maybe Paul wanted the Colossians and the Laodiceans to trade copies of his letters. It turns out that the adjacent town of Colossae also has a bearing on our understanding of this letter to the Laodiceans. (3:14-21)

The church in Laodicea was like the culture around it in two ways:

First, the church resembled the city's water supply. Laodicea's water was piped overland from the hot springs of Hierapolis, and the cold springs of Colossae, and so the city ended up with a disgusting lukewarm water coming out of both supply pipes. Likewise the church was not useful to Christ because it wasn't hot (a good, healing water) or cold (a good, refreshing water). They were a bland mix of Christian truth and the self-sufficient culture, likely to be spat out of the mouth.

(Please note, Jesus was not saying He would rather they were antagonistic toward Him – cold – rather than spiritually struggling – lukewarm. This idea is often preached, but it contradicts the biblical teaching that Jesus does not despise the weak of faith. See Isaiah 42:1-4. Both hot and cold water were good things, but the lukewarm version of either was disgusting. Jesus wants His followers to be His followers, not a bland blend of faith diluted by culture.)

Second, the church reflected the city's self-sufficient complacency. They thought they had all that they needed, for they were rich and well resourced. But Jesus had been left out of the church. He was standing on the outside and knocking! (see 3:17-20)

The description of Christ at the start of this letter portrays Him as consistent and certain, the key figure in creation and history. (3:14) Self-sufficiency on the part of believers seems so ridiculous in light of who Jesus is, not to mention where He is – on the heavenly throne (3:21). How can we be self-sufficient and ignore Christ who should be the focus of our devotion and attention?

And the promise to the overcomer? Jesus, the central figure in history, will share His throne with the overcomer. (3:21-22)

What does this mean for us today? We have a tendency to leave Christ out of the picture and pursue our own tepid self-sufficiency that is so repugnant to Him. Christ is actually the central figure in all of history, yet He stands at the door of the church knocking and seeking fellowship with us. On top of all this, if He plans to share His throne with us in the future, then surely we should open the door and enjoy dependent fellowship with Him now? We could start by telling Him how much we need Him today!

The majestic, powerful, impressive, fall-flat-on-your-face-if-he-walks-in Jesus wants intimacy with His church! He is ready to come close and fellowship with you now. He is also looking forward to fellowshipping with you later, face to face. If you have read this far, then hopefully your heart is well and truly ready for a wedding, the great wedding ... the wedding of Christ and His bride!

24 The Wedding!

• REVELATION

The end of the creation of God was to provide a spouse for his Son Jesus Christ that might enjoy him and on whom he might pour forth his love. And the end of all things in providence are to make way for the exceeding expressions of Christ's close and intimate union with, and high and glorious enjoyment of, him and to bring this to pass. And therefore the last thing and the issue of all things is the marriage of the Lamb. … The wedding feast is eternal; and the love and joys, the songs, entertainments and glories of the wedding never will be ended. It will be an everlasting wedding day.[1]

JONATHAN EDWARDS

1. Jonathan Edwards, 'Miscellanies' (No. 702) in *Works,* vol. 18, p. 298.

Heaven is not heaven without Christ. It is better to be in any place with Christ than to be in heaven itself without him. All delicacies without Christ are but as a funeral banquet ... . What is all without Christ? I say the joys of heaven are not the joys of heaven without Christ; he is the very heaven of heaven ... . True love is carried to the person. It is adulterous love, to love the thing, or the gift, more than the person ... . To be with Christ is to be at the spring-head of all happiness. It is to be in our proper element. Every creature thinks itself best in its own element, that is the place it thrives in, and enjoys its happiness in; now Christ is the element of a Christian. Again, it is far better, because to be with Christ is to have the marriage consummate. Is not marriage better than the contract? Is not home better than absence? To be with Christ is to be at home.[2]

RICHARD SIBBES

The last book of the Bible is the only one that specifically claims to offer a blessing to the person who reads it. Sadly, many don't. After all, we hear people warning of how difficult it is to interpret this kind of book, or we see some who seem to obsess with this book and never look at the rest of the Bible. Either way, we feel safer staying at a reasonable distance.

Our goal in this chapter is not to discuss the right way to interpret the middle chapters of Revelation, but rather to see the thrilling finale to the great threads that have woven their way through the Bible, and also through this particular book.

The centre of the Revelation presents a frightening array of evil forces. In chapter 12, for instance, there is a hideous

---

2. Richard Sibbes, 'Christ is Best' in *Works,* volume 1, p. 339.

red dragon prepared to devour the Christ child, but he is thwarted. The dragon is depicted in raging battle with the forces of heaven with an army of angels at his command. But this dragon, Satan, ends up being thrown to the earth. So the earth becomes a battleground with Satan's evil forces on the attack. Then in chapter 13 we encounter a blasphemous beast rising up from the sea, and another beast that comes from the earth. This is hell's great assault against God's purposes on earth; who will win?

In chapter 14 the scene shifts from the battlefield of the earth to the peace of Mount Zion. This heavenly peace is neither tranquil, nor dull. It is a dynamic and vibrant, yet somehow intimate scene that is presented. The Lamb of God is with the 144,000 faithful witnesses (see Rev. 7 for their introduction) – who are marked as belonging to God, and they are singing. But don't miss that the first voice described is God's – forever the great initiator. Many waters, loud thunder, many harpists … how do you describe the great voice of God? And His people are singing in response to Him a new song. They were uniquely qualified, by God's redeeming work, to sing this particular song to their God. John goes on to describe the purity of these people in distinctly marital terms. These virgins, redeemed by the blood of the Lamb, followed faithfully after Him.

Just a few verses later, there is a loud voice warning the people on earth. (see 14:6-20) The angel messenger has an eternal gospel to proclaim, but he is followed by another angel who proclaims the downfall of Babylon the Great – the personified city of godless mankind who made all the nations drunk on the wine of her sexual immorality. What a contrast to the virgin purity of the redeemed in heaven! But now there is good news on the earth; Babylon the Great is fallen! Her deceptive whoring is over. The next chapters will finally unravel the confusion that has felt so unremitting since the very earliest chapters of Genesis: two great cities, made up of the people in this world. There is Babylon, with a fist shaking toward heaven, forever in opposition to God. And there is Zion, which will ultimately be the bride in the great wedding. It is time for the ages-long battle to be resolved; it is time for a harvest, and time for wrath to be unleashed!

The Great Demise

Revelation progresses through three sets of seven judgments. Earlier there are the seven seals, then the seven trumpets, and now in chapters 15 and 16 we read of the seven bowls of wrath to be poured out. Wherever we might choose to place these events in time, it is clear that the intensity is rising to fever pitch. Time is ticking down and ultimately Satan's world system is facing absolute demise.

As chapter 15 begins we see the the seven bowls of God's wrath are given to seven angels coming out of the sanctuary, to a chorus of praise from the redeemed. The destruction caused as the seven bowls are poured out is breathtaking. The people of the earth endure agony, sea life is killed, fresh water is turned to blood – a fitting drink for a world that has spilled the blood of God's precious people. The sun grows fierce, yet people do not repent. The kingdom of the beast is plunged into darkness, and still the people curse God. Massive demonic-inspired armies are described assembling for battle. And finally, the seventh bowl brings storms like Israel experienced at Mt Sinai back in the book of Exodus, and earthquakes. As cities collapse, one great city is exposed and vulnerable. Chapters 15, and now 16, have turned the spotlight squarely on the great prostitute city, Babylon. Her fall is the focus of the next two chapters – here comes the ultimate demise.

The angel turns John's attention (and therefore ours) to the focal point of the judgment. The counterpoint to the bride of Christ is 'the great prostitute who is seated on many waters, with whom the kings of the earth have committed sexual immorality, and with the wine of whose sexual immorality the dwellers on earth have become drunk'. (17:1-2) Here comes the climax to the great biblical theme of spiritual adultery and religious whoredom. So the reader sees a gaudily regaled harlot riding a scarlet beast, holding aloft her golden cup 'full of abominations and the impurities of her sexual immorality'. (17:4) Her identity is no secret, it is tattooed on her forehead, 'Babylon the great, mother of prostitutes and of earth's abominations.' She was drunk with the blood of God's people. (17:5-6) This nightmarish image should leave us speechless with disgust.

The passage goes on to explain the political context in which this woman existed. The political alliances of nations described here ultimately arm themselves against the Lamb– who will conquer them (see 17:7-14). The bottom line is that the woman is the great city of Babylon, influential over all human authorities (17:18). Everything that is hideous and unfaithful to God is wrapped up in this drunk harlot revelling with the kings of the earth. What is to become of her? Chapter 17 asks the question. Chapter 18 answers in no uncertain terms.

Fallen! Fallen is Babylon the great! (18:2) All the leaders of humanity may have drunk of her immorality and committed immorality with her, but the time has come for her demise (18:3). So God's people are finally called to leave her and separate themselves as judgment approaches. The city celebrates her significance, while judgment falls on her from God (18:7-8). As the smoke rises, her lovers will mourn her demise; the kings and the merchants are among the chief mourners, for unfaithfulness to God has always manifested in lust for power and lust for possessions (18:9-19).

In a great demonstration of termination, an angel throws a great millstone into the sea. This is how Babylon will be finished! Absolutely, completely, suddenly, overwhelmingly – this is total and final judgment. So the angel describes the end of the bazaar that was Babylon. No more music, or craft, or work, or – remember Jeremiah? – no more voice of the bridegroom and bride! (18:21-24)

What a comfort to know that the world system – with its overt antagonism against God – will be shut down completely! This system is so evil that it can only be described in terms of prostitution, lust and wanton infidelity toward a loving God. Oh, how God's heart must have broken throughout the ages over the hatred of humanity toward Him. It is hard to fathom that the good God of the Bible could be rejected in favour of the empty pursuit of an ungodly world where humans are gods, and things are gods, and most importantly, God is not God! Even in light of the Father's great patience, and the sacrifice of the Lamb of God, still humanity continues to spurn Him. In a charade of security and success, as stable as the candy floss in a fairground, their spiritual adultery promised everything but delivered nothing. God is patient, longing for all to turn away from this emptiness and be His, but the rejection cannot go on forever. And so, with hearts aching for the miserable world around us, we find ourselves relieved that the adulterous God-hating system is finally judged.

Perhaps we let slip a little 'hallelujah.' Heaven erupts with hallelujahs at the final demise of Babylon the Great;

now let ambiguity cease and victorious celebration begin! Chapter 19 …

The Great Victory

God's victory and judgment are celebrated with a heavenly hallelujah chorus (19:1-10). God has judged the great prostitute! (19:2) And so the hallelujahs keep sounding forth, angels joining with the great multitude of the redeemed, now able, together, to roar with a voice something like God's own, crying out to Him in celebration and praise! Hallelujah! We will never know the fullness of that great cry in this life, although this life is what creates the inner thirst for that moment to come! Now that the great prostitute is finished, immediately the cry goes out, 'It is time!' 'The time has come!' It is time for the marriage of the Lamb and the bride is very ready for it! She is prepared, dressed in the finest of linens, bright and pure, which are the righteous deeds of the saints; the purity of righteous deeds lived out in the darkness of this world will shine as the greatest wedding dress on that glorious day! (19:6-8)

The time has come, the bride is ready, but where is the heroic groom? Suddenly heaven tears open like paper and out bursts a charging white horse. The heroic groom is riding the charger! This is Faithful, this is True, and He is ready to defeat the foe of His Father and the enemy of His bride. The groom has eyes like flames of fire – He is coming to judge all sin. He has many crowns – for He has all authority. His clothes are dipped in blood – for He defeats the armies amassed against Him. What a sight He will be to a world that has long lived in hatred of this One they now see! He comes, He strikes down, He rules, 'He treads the winepress of the fury of the wrath of God the Almighty!' (19:15) This hero, everyone needs to know, is the very King of kings, and Lord of lords. This is the groom come to defeat the enemy and marry the bride!

The first feast is for the birds of the air, vultures ready to tear flesh, for this is a feast of defeated enemies. (19:17-21) The next chapter finishes the great demise – not just the demise of the emissaries of Satan who have made the earth such a place of darkness, but the demise of Satan himself. One last deception, one last attack, one last opportunity to see that his fight against God is forever futile, and the armies gather against God and His anointed one last time. God laughs at this kind of nonsense (see Ps. 2). And what happens to His enemies? 'Fire came down from heaven and consumed them.' (20:9) Opposing God has always been futile; then everyone will know it. So there is judgment of those whose names are not in the Lamb's book of life, and all the unredeemed of history are fully judged. Sobering, but a precursor for what is to follow. Is that a wedding march starting to sound in the distance?

The Great Wedding

The stage is quickly set. This is not a wedding in a church, for the bride *is* the church. This is not an outdoor wedding, for this world is too marred by the previous occupants. In quick time the earth is purged with fire and we have a new heaven and a new earth. A new stage, for the culmination of all of history. The music now rings out triumphantly as the heavenly doors open and the bride enters the scene … she is the holy city, the new Jerusalem, coming down the heavenly aisle to complete the story of history. What will it be like to be part of the great climax of human history, of God's story, of the great wedding? On that day, we will know. The bride will be prepared and adorned for her groom.

Then a voice from heaven speaks, and the immediate declaration is that biggest of big ideas; it is a declaration of divine intent that speaks of divine marriage and true union. Let everything in the new creation gaze in wonder: now the 'dwelling place of God is with man. He will dwell with them, and they will be his people, and God himself will be with them as their God.' (21:3) God wants to be with His people, in their midst, united in the most glorious union, dwelling together in divine matrimony.

The union of God and humanity begins with a moment of tenderness, 'He will wipe away every tear from their eyes, and death shall be no more, neither shall there be mourning, nor crying, nor pain anymore, for the former things have passed away.' (21:4) This is a new life, forever changed, and tears have no place here.

What comes immediately after the description of the wedding? God speaks, first proclaiming a new day and then declaring, 'It is done!' This is that great moment for which the whole Bible, and the whole of human history, and every believer's heart, has forever longed. The wedding union between Christ and His church is not just an image. It is a reality. It is not a means to an end. It *is* the end. This is the great theme of the Bible from cover to cover, from wedding to wedding, from the Garden of Eden to the New Creation. (21:5-8)

John needed help to take in all that he had seen. So one of the angels invited him to visit the New Jerusalem, described as 'the Bride, the wife of the Lamb.' (21:9) This city is holy, set apart for God. This bride radiates the wonder of her groom – for it is the glory of God that is the holiness and the purity and the righteousness of the city. We will never stand before God in our own righteousness, for we will be forever clothed in His own righteousness. How can that be described? Well, 'like a most rare jewel, like a jasper, clear as crystal.' (21:11) John does a great job trying, but it feels like he can't find words for it. He describes the beauty and purity of the bride, the security of the bride, then the unity of the bride (Israel and Church). This unity is pictured as the gates and the foundations of the city (twelve tribes, twelve apostles) (21:11-14). These structures are described as being made of precious stones, each of which refracts every beam of glorious light into a spectrum of dazzling beauty (21:15-21).

And John's tour of the city concludes with some key insights. There is no temple there, because the temple was supposed to be a place for God's presence to dwell in the midst of His people (21:22) Now there is no need for a shelter, no limits, no required sacrificial processes, because God the Father and the Lamb can be the temple in the city. There is no sun or moon, for the light that radiates is the resplendent glory of God – the dynamic energy of the relationship between Father and Son lighting the bride with whom He is now united and indwelling! And there is no night, so no fear, no doubts, no distance with the spouse disappearing as in Song of Songs. No night implies no threat – which is reinforced by the fact that nothing unclean of any sort can ever enter the city! (21:22-27)

In the midst of the city there is the water of life, flowing out from God's throne, with the tree of life lining both sides of the great river. This city is more alive than any city has ever been. In the old world, each city would try to encourage life with busy central areas, buzzing commerce, even cultivated parks. This new city is truly alive, because God Himself is at the centre and life is flowing out as a river, and the tree of life is restored. Now people have no appetite for sin, so death does not need to be a feature anymore. Now people will see the face of the Lamb and worship Him, and there will never be night again. (22:1-5)

The Great Cry

John saw the conclusion for which our souls yearn every day – the great demise of the hideous alternative to a marital, faithful God, and the great wedding of God's Christ and His bride. That picture is painted marvellously before our eyes; so our hearts can cry out with those that have rung down through the ages in response to His promise to come soon (22:7, 12) … 'Come!' (22:17) This is the great cry of the Spirit – the one who forever points our hearts to Christ. This is the great cry of the bride – the beloved souls who long to see the face of their Christ. 'Come!'

Jesus ends the book of Revelation, and the Bible, with 'Surely I am coming soon.' And with one voice we join with John in crying out, 'Amen! Come, Lord Jesus!' (22:20)

Conclusion

May the grace of Christ our Saviour,
And the Father's boundless love,
With the Holy Spirit's favour,
Rest upon us from above!

Thus may we abide in union
With each other in the Lord;
And possess, in sweet communion,
Joys which earth cannot afford.[1]

JOHN NEWTON
May the Grace of Christ Our Saviour

1. John Newton, 'May the Grace of Christ Our Saviour', Hymn, 1779.

The Bible begins with a wedding. This is what it is all about. Adam, the gardener, waxed eloquent praising his bride, but the marriage turned sour.

The Bible depicts a history full to the brim with troubled marriages. The great heroes of the faith struggled on a human level. Abraham gave his wife away more than once. King David took another man's wife.

The great story of God's marriage to Israel struggled on a spiritual level. During the honeymoon, in the wilderness, Israel gave herself to whoredom and cast off all restraint before a different god. The pattern continued. The nation was spiritually promiscuous time and again, time without number. Under every green tree, on every high hill, in every hotel room in the city, she was unfaithful to God. But what a God she had who was so faithful to her!

He should have cast her off, and the cosmos would have cried out its support. Yet God proceeded to send His Son into the world of sinful rebels. This was the Son for whom God planned to call a bride. But this bride was one for whom the Son would have to give His life. God could not offer a half-hearted marriage of convenience. He could not just give a token status change to a people whose hearts were opposed to Him. He had to give everything, because He had to change everything. He had to win the bride's stony heart.

He gave His Son to woo an uninterested bride, drawing our hearts to a love that we have never been able to muster, even for ourselves. He gave His Son to pay the bride price, to wipe away the guilty record of each rebel human. He gave His Spirit to unite each one to His Son in spiritual matrimony, presenting us holy and spotless, through the remarkable act of transformation that only God can do.

In this world we struggle to believe that I am really my beloved's and He is really mine. But it is so, and the Spirit is given to us to assure us of God's love, and of our union with Christ. We aren't just legally married, we are in a close, intimate relationship. (At this stage, united in Spirit and betrothed, for the wedding is still future.) It isn't just a metaphor; it is the greatest of spiritual realities. And all creation is longing for the day when this present reality will be made complete.

The new creation, the beautified bride, the victorious Groom, the glorious wedding. Stirring and tender, the union will mean forever togetherness with the God who made us and gives us life itself. As Ray Ortlund puts it so beautifully, 'This perfect union brings together a triumphant Lamb and a pure Bride beyond the reach of hell and sin. ... she has been purified of all adulterous inclinations and is finally ready to give herself fully to her one Husband, and to no other, for ever.'[2]

This life will only be a memory as we sit at His table. 'He brought me to the banqueting table, and His banner over me is love.' (Song of Songs 2:4) Love that shares, that talks, that laughs. Love that cares, that listens, that celebrates. Love that can only be experienced in marriage to a good spouse, will be known by each one of us together in our marriage to the most perfect spouse – the very Son of God Himself.

That great day stands before us as the hope to which we are called. Yet it is not simply a day out there in the future. We are called into union with Christ today, by His Spirit. On that day we will have so much more because we will see Him face to face and we will be freed from the sin of our

---

2. Ray Ortlund, Jr., *God's Unfaithful Wife,* p. 163.

bodies and this world. But in another sense we will never have more than what we already have *now* in our union with Christ! (Although I suspect we will gradually grasp its reality more and more then.) We are invited to be united to Christ today. What a glorious privilege!

May we never dull the wonder of the great storyline of the Bible by turning true union with Christ by the Spirit into simply a status change, a legal arrangement and a mere metaphor. Instead, let every moment in the Bible awaken a longing in your heart. Let every moment of relational delight in this life stir a longing in your heart. Let every disappointment or hurt in this life, every injustice and every sniff of hell's schemes ignite a passion in your heart. Let every earthly minute that God providentially gives you swell a passion in your heart for Christ Himself, and for that day when every battle will be over, every sin will be past, every doubt will be put to rest, and every enemy will be put down. May God, by His Spirit, who tells us of God's love and Christ's excellency, stir a passion for that day when our faith will be sight, and the gaze of our eyes will join the gaze of our hearts, fixed on the Christ who is forever ours.

Maybe in that day, as the feasting continues and God celebrates over His people, maybe Christ will take His bride in His arms for the first face-to-face dance. Maybe in that moment, as all else fades to a blur and there is nothing but Him, we will find ourselves gripped in an embrace both gentle and strong. Maybe in that moment, the church, held by Christ, will be led by Christ in a dazzling twirl asking only that we abandon ourselves to His lead, to trust, to enjoy, and to accept His love. And maybe in that moment we will realize that this is the first dance face-to-face, but it is not the first dance. Maybe only then will we realise that the dance began back in this world and in this life. And maybe only then will we realise how perfect was His grip, and how deliberate was His lead. Maybe only then will we realise just how united we were already, by the Spirit, to our beloved in this life. The wedding is still to come, and an eternity in the world of love that is heaven. But the proposal is behind us already, and today, by His Spirit, we are already united to Him. The music is already playing in our hearts, if only we stop to listen. The dance has already begun. The invitation is already in place, 'Follow me.'

So with the proposal behind us and the wedding still future, our hearts plead with our Lord to finish His new creation. We long for Him to return and never leave again! What a day that will be when He makes us pure and spotless, clothed in the greater glory still to come. In that day we will take our place as the bride of the Lamb, and we will cast our crowns before Him. And, before Him, we truly will be lost in wonder, love and praise.

Sources Cited

Billings, J. Todd. *Union with Christ: Reframing Theology and Ministry for the Church.* Grand Rapids, MI: Baker Academic, 2011.

Boston, Thomas. *Human Nature in Its Four Fold State.* Originally published Bungay, 1812. Carlisle, PA: The Banner of Truth Trust, 1964, 1989.

Burroughs, Jeremiah. *An Exposition of Hosea*, Edinburgh: James Nichol, 1863.

Chalmers, Thomas. *Posthumous Works of Thomas Chalmers*, Vol. 3. T. Constable, 1852.

Calvin, John. *Institutes of the Christian Religion*, ed. John T. McNeil, trans. Ford Lewis Battles, Library of Christian Classics, Vols. 20-21. Philadelphia: Westminster, 1960.

Eaton, John. *The Honey-Combe of Free Justification.* London, 1642, edited by Robert Lancaster.

Edwards, Jonathan. *Religious Affections, Works,* volume 2. Yale, 2009.

_____. *Miscellanies,* in *The Works of Jonathan Edwards,* volume 18. New Haven, CT: Yale University Press, 1957-2009.

Fairbairn, Donald. *Life in the Trinity: An Introduction to Theology with the Help of the Church Fathers.* Downers Grove, IL: IVP, 2009.

Fairbairn, Patrick. *Exposition of Ezekiel.* Edinburgh: T&T Clark, 1855, reprint 1960.

Fisher, Edward. *The Marrow of Modern Divinity.* Christian Focus, 2009, originally published in 1724.

Goodwin, Thomas. *The Heart of Christ.* Edinburgh: The Banner of Truth Trust, 2011.

Johnson, Marcus Peter. *One With Christ: An Evangelical Theology of Salvation.* Wheaton, IL: Crossway, 2013.

Kaiser Jr., Walter C. *The Promise Plan of God.* Zondervan, 2008.

Lewis, C.S. *Perelandra.* Originally published in 1944. Scribner Classics Edition, 1996.

_____. 'The Weight of Glory.' Published in *Theology,* November 1941.

Lloyd-Jones, D. Martyn. *Romans: Exposition of Chapter 8:5-17, The Sons of God.* Edinburgh: The Banner of Truth Trust, 1974.

Luther, Martin. *Lectures on Galatians,* 1535 edition in *Luther's Works,* vol. 26. Concordia, 1963.

Luther, Martin. 'The Freedom of a Christian' in *Three Treatises*. Fortress Press, 1943.

Mead, Peter. *Pleased To Dwell: A Biblical Introduction to the Incarnation*. Christian Focus: 2014.

Moo, Douglas J. *The Letter of James*, The Pillar New Testament Commentary. Leicester, England: Apollos, 2000.

Murray, John. *Redemption: Accomplished and Applied*. Edinburgh: The Banner of Truth Trust, 1977, originally published in 1955.

Newbigin, Lesslie. *The Light Has Come*. Grand Rapids, Eerdmans: 1982.

Ortlund, Dane. *Edwards on the Christian Life*. Wheaton, IL: Crossway, 2014.

Ortlund Jr., Ray. *God's Unfaithful Wife: A Biblical Theology of Spiritual Adultery*. Downers Grove, IL: IVP Apollos, 1996.

Packer, J.I. 'Justification.' In *Evangelical Dictionary of Theology*. Edited by Walter Elwell. Grand Rapids: Baker, 2001.

Reeves, Michael. *The Good God*. Milton Keynes: Paternoster, 2012.

————. *Christ Our Life*. Milton Keynes: Paternoster, 2014.

Scougal, Henry. *The Life of God in the Soul of Man*. Boston, Nichols & Notes: 1868. (Written originally in 1670s)

Scrivener, Glen. *321: The Story of God, the World, and You*. 10Publishing, 2014.

Sibbes, Richard. 'A Description of Christ,' *The Complete Works of Richard Sibbes*, vol.1. Edinburgh, The Banner of Truth Trust, 1973.

————. 'Christ is Best,' *The Complete Works of Richard Sibbes*, vol.1. Edinburgh, The Banner of Truth Trust, 1973.

_____. 'A Glance of Heaven,' *The Complete Works of Richard Sibbes*, vol.4. Edinburgh: The Banner of Truth Trust, 1973.

_____. 'Fountains Opened,' in Works vol. 5. Edinburgh, The Banner of Truth Trust, 1973.

_____. 'The Successful Seeker,' in Works vol. 6. Edinburgh, The Banner of Truth Trust, 1973.

Spurgeon, Charles Haddon. 'Perseverence in Holiness,' in *Metropolitan Tabernacle Pulpit*, Vol. 35. Pasadena, TX: Pilgrim, 1975.

James Stewart, *Man in Christ*. 1935; reprinted, Vancouver: Regent College, 2002.

Hymns

Newton, John. 'May the Grace of Christ Our Saviour', Hymn, 1779.

Robinson, Robert. 'Come, Thou Fount of Every Blessing', Hymn, 1758.

A. B. Simpson, 'I Am Crucified With Christ', Hymn.

Wesley, Charles. 'And Can It Be?', Hymn, 1738.

_____. 'Hark the Herald Angels Sing', Hymn, 1739.

_____. 'Love Divine, All Loves Excelling', Hymn, 1747.

_____. 'Jesus Lover of My Soul', Hymn, 1740.

*Also available
from this author...*

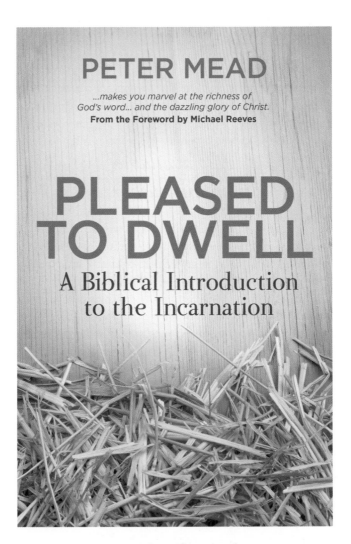

PETER MEAD

...makes you marvel at the richness of God's word... and the dazzling glory of Christ.
From the Foreword by Michael Reeves

PLEASED TO DWELL

A Biblical Introduction to the Incarnation

ISBN 978-1-78191-426-7

Pleased to Dwell
A Biblical Introduction to the Incarnation
PETER MEAD

At the centre of heaven is Christ, lovingly adored as the forever Lord of all. At the centre of Christmas is Christ, frail and cradled in the tender arms of a young mother. How can the two be put together? Heavenly glory and human frailty? That is the real wonder of Christmas. *Pleased to Dwell* is an energetic biblical introduction to Christmas. It is an invitation to ponder the Incarnation, and a God who was please to dwell with us.

Building anticipation with the great themes of the Old Testament, enjoying the remarkably distinct birth narratives of Matthew, then Luke, before surveying some great New Testament passages, Pleased to Dwell is an engaging introduction to the wonder of the Word becoming flesh and dwelling among us. This book offers a wealth of ideas for preachers, an easy access mini-reference tool for Bible students, and an enjoyable cover-to-cover read for everyone. Twenty-four short chapters would make a great advent devotional, but this book is not just for Christmas. God's Son stepped into our world and that changes every day of the year!

> What a really useful resource! As I read through it, I found that ideas for carol service talks just kept leaping off its pages.
>
> Rico Tice
> Author, Christianity Explored & Associate Minister
> All Souls Church, Langham Place, London

> In this book we see the profound truths of the incarnation presented in a way that makes the Bible and its truth come alive. And, best of all, it is presented in an engaging style that makes it accessible to ordinary laypersons.
>
> Ajith Fernando
> Teaching Director, Youth for Christ, Sri Lanka

Christian Focus Publications

Our mission statement –

STAYING FAITHFUL

In dependence upon God we seek to impact the world through literature faithful to His infallible Word, the Bible. Our aim is to ensure that the Lord Jesus Christ is presented as the only hope to obtain forgiveness of sin, live a useful life and look forward to heaven with Him.

Our Books are published in four imprints:

CHRISTIAN
FOCUS

popular works including biographies, commentaries, basic doctrine and Christian living.

CHRISTIAN
HERITAGE

books representing some of the best material from the rich heritage of the church.

MENTOR

books written at a level suitable for Bible College and seminary students, pastors, and other serious readers. The imprint includes commentaries, doctrinal studies, examination of current issues and church history.

CF4•K

children's books for quality Bible teaching and for all age groups: Sunday school curriculum, puzzle and activity books; personal and family devotional titles, biographies and inspirational stories – because you are never too young to know Jesus!

Christian Focus Publications Ltd,
Geanies House, Fearn, Ross-shire,
IV20 1TW, Scotland, United Kingdom.
www.christianfocus.com